C000040074

PERSPECTIVES ON EDUCATION POLICY

Institute of Education

University of London

Ability Grouping in Schools: A literature review

SUSAN HALLAM

© Institute of Education 2002

Institute of Education University of London
20 Bedford Way
London WC1H 0AL

Pursuing Excellence in Education

British Library Cataloguing in Publication Data:
A catalogue record for this publication is
available from the British Library

ISBN 0-85473-659-X

Produced in Great Britain by
RICOH Document Services
Institute of Education University of London

CONTENTS

Foreword

The issue of ability grouping has been an ever-present concern almost since the beginning of educational research. Often presented as a matter related to the best way to organise teaching, it has a much broader significance and is often the focus of bitter struggle. Ability grouping rests on particular assumptions about the nature of ability and its measurement and relates to the ways in which scarce educational resources in schools are distributed. As Susan Hallam's work points out, ability grouping is also central to the economy of student esteem and struggles over access to success roles and routes in schools. The impact of and consequences for those students deemed 'low ability', the academic, social and personal outcomes of grouping by ability, are usually untoward.

Nonetheless, UK primary and secondary schools – partly at government and parental behest, partly in anticipation of 'market forces' – are currently moving in large numbers back to systems of setting and streaming, which had been previously abandoned. To a great extent these moves are taking place in ignorance of or directly against the findings of extensive research.

This review of ability grouping research is exhaustive, topical and of crucial educational importance both for social justice and for raising achievement.

STEPHEN J. BALL
Karl Mannheim Professor of Sociology of Education
Institute of Education

1

Introduction

Ability grouping has been the subject of research for most of the 20th century, since Whipple carried out a study of the effects of special class placement on a group of high-aptitude fifth and sixth graders in the USA in 1919. Since then hundreds of studies have been undertaken and there have been many literature reviews and syntheses of research findings, including several undertaken recently in the UK (Hallam and Tountounji, 1996a; 1996b; Harlen and Malcolm, 1997; Sukhnandan and Lee, 1998; Ireson and Hallam, 1999).

Despite this ever-increasing body of evidence, the field has been characterised by controversy and polemic. There are several reasons for this. Firstly, there has been no clear definition of the meaning of 'effective' in relation to educational outcomes. Effectiveness may be judged in relation to academic, social and personal outcomes for pupils. Contrasting types of grouping can therefore be judged as effective by the adoption of different criteria of effectiveness. Secondly, the research undertaken has rarely been able to consider the various consequences of different types of grouping together. Conclusions have thus had to be drawn across studies adopting different methodologies, which has made definitive comparison difficult. Thirdly, and perhaps most importantly, different types of grouping seem to benefit different groups of pupils. Streaming and setting tend to benefit the more able, whereas mixed-ability structures tend to benefit the less able. The type of pupil grouping which is adopted is therefore underpinned by different philosophical values. Because of this, policy decisions about pupil grouping have often been based on ideological principles rather than educational ones.

Underlying policies of selective education, streaming, banding and setting are fundamental assumptions relating to the nature of intelligence. Historically, the IQ view of intelligence has tended to be related to an assumption that intelligence is both genetically determined and immutable (Ceci, 1990). However, recent research indicates that the genetic basis of intelligence is complex, depending on the contribution of many rather than single genes (Plomin, 1986). Further, geneticists now view behaviour as reflecting the functioning of the whole organism, being dynamic and changing in response to the environment (Plomin and Thompson, 1993). Even research using traditional statistical techniques acknowledges an important role for the environment, heritability estimates for general intelligence being in the region of 50 per cent. Existing evidence also indicates large discrepancies between heritability estimates for specific cognitive abilities and school achievement, implying that other factors are implicated in school performance.

Taken together, these studies acknowledge a crucial role for the environment in the development of intelligence. This is further supported by evidence that IQ scores can be improved by training (Feuerstein *et al.*, 1980; Sternberg and Weil, 1980) and are influenced by the length of time spent in school (Ceci, 1990).

Recent conceptualisations of intelligence acknowledge its complexity. Gardner (1993; 1999) proposes a theory of multiple intelligences, including linguistic, logico-mathematical, spatial, musical, bodily-kinaesthetic, interpersonal, intrapersonal, naturalist and spiritual/existential. Sternberg (1984) has developed a triarchic theory that considers intelligence in three ways. Firstly, in terms of the internal world of the individual, or the mental mechanisms that underlie intelligent behaviour; secondly, in terms of the external world of the individual, or the use of these mental mechanisms in everyday life in order to attain an intelligent fit to the environment; and thirdly, in terms of experience, or the mediating role of one's passage through life between the internal and external worlds of the individual.

Ceci (1990) proposes a bio-ecological theory which, like Gardner's, is based on multiple potentials. The theory stresses the importance of context, including motivational forces, the social and physical aspects of a particular learning environment or task and the knowledge domain in which the task is embedded. Knowledge and aptitude are viewed as fundamentally inseparable; learning therefore acquires a crucial role in the development of intelligence. Other researchers have suggested that even within single-subject domains, individuals attaining similar overall levels of expertise can exhibit differing patterns of attainment which may be achieved by differing processing styles (Sloboda *et al.*, 1994; Hallam, 1998). This research not only raises issues regarding the notion of a single unitary intelligence but questions assumptions about the unitary nature of 'ability', even within single-subject domains.

The unitary view of intelligence proposes that IQ scores predict learning outcomes in school and subsequent success in employment. However, correlations of IQ with school grades vary a great deal, although they are usually within the range of 0.4 to 0.6 (Block and Dworkin, 1976; Brody, 1985). This represents 36 per cent of the variance, leaving much unexplained. There is also an increasing body of research indicating mismatches between IQ scores and performance on tasks requiring complex cognitive skills (Ceci, 1990). Job status, because of its relationship with academic attainment, is related to IQ scores, but the relationship with actual work performance is very low (Jenson, 1970; Ceci, 1990). Researchers now acknowledge that learning outcomes and performance depend on the complex interactions of many factors, including the characteristics of the learning situation, motivation, effort, belief in the possibility of success, opportunity, knowledge of learning strategies, self-awareness and prior knowledge, in addition to ability (Carroll, 1963; Entwistle, 1981; Biggs and Moore, 1993; Hallam and Ireson, 1999). Recently, Goleman (1996) has suggested that what he describes as emotional intelligence is more important than measures of cognitive ability in predicting success in life. Overall, intelligence as traditionally conceived is now believed to play a relatively small part in an individual's success in life.

Cross-cultural studies comparing educational systems in Japan and Taiwan with those in the USA suggest that the Western stress on ability grouping minimises the importance of student, teacher and parental effort. The concept of differential ability sets a ceiling on what can be expected from a child. In Japan and Taiwan, pupils, with support from parents and teachers, are expected to put in additional effort if they are not successful (George, 1989; Stevenson and Lee, 1990). No one expects pupils to be removed from the classroom for special interventions or to make it easier to move ahead. There is no ability grouping in state schools prior to tenth grade in Japanese schools. The school day is longer and people are encouraged to work hard. In recent years, increased attainment in literacy and numeracy at primary level, where the majority of pupils have attained levels initially seen as 'average', supports the idea that the Western emphasis on ability may serve to lower our expectations of what pupils can achieve.

Current thinking about the nature of intelligence, the many factors which affect learning outcomes and the evidence indicating the importance of effort indicate a need for grouping structures within schools which increase pupil motivation and are sufficiently flexible to meet pupils' ever-changing needs. As early as 1931, Turney outlined the advantages and disadvantages of systems of streaming, banding or setting. These are set out in Table 1.1. As this literature review will reveal, the evidence from more recent research indicates an even more complex picture.

TABLE 1.1: PERCEIVED ADVANTAGES AND DISADVANTAGES OF STRUCTURED ABILITY GROUPING

Advantages	Disadvantages
• permits pupils to make progress commensurate with their abilities	• slow pupils need the presence of the able students to stimulate them and encourage them
• makes possible an adaption of the technique of instruction to the needs of the group	• a stigma is attached to low sections, discouraging the pupils in these sections
• reduces failure	• teachers are unable, or do not have time, to differentiate the work for different levels of ability
• helps to maintain interest and incentive, because bright students are not bored by the participation of the dull	• teachers object to the slower groups.
• encourages slower pupils to participate more because they are not eclipsed by those who are much brighter	
• makes teaching easier	
• makes possible individual instruction to small slow groups.	

Derived from Turney (1931)

ABILITY GROUPING PRACTICES IN THE UK PAST AND PRESENT

There is a long tradition of structured ability grouping in the UK. Following the separation of the old 'elementary' schools into primary and secondary schools, the Primary School Report of 1930 recommended that children in primary schools should be grouped in classes according to ability (streaming) where numbers allowed (Hadow Report, 1930). In practice, however, most primary schools were too small to implement streaming.

In 1944, the Butler Education Act established the need for ability grouping to ensure effective selection for different types of schooling at secondary level. Following this, the practice of streaming became widespread in larger primary schools throughout the 1940s and 1950s as pupils competed for grammar school places. In the 1960s it began to decline in popularity as research showed that it had no significant effect on overall attainment, and had negative social consequences for certain pupils (Jackson, 1964; Barker Lunn, 1970). By the 1970s, surveys of primary school organisation found that of those schools that were large enough to stream, only about 20 per cent chose to do so (Bealing, 1972; DES, 1978). At this time there was also a general trend in educational values towards a more child-centred approach, with emphasis on the overall development of the individual rather than on academic achievement, and on equality of opportunity rather than the pursuit of excellence. The Plowden Report (1967) reflected this trend, and was influential in encouraging schools towards 'unstreaming'. With the demise of the 11+ examination and the spread of comprehensive secondary education, mixed-ability classes became the norm in primary schools, and there was a move away from formal 'traditional' teaching methods. In a survey of primary schools in two LEAs in the 1990s, Lee and Croll (1995) reported that less than 3 per cent of the total adopted streaming by ability. Streaming as a form of school organisation in primary schools had almost disappeared.

During the 1990s, the main educational emphasis was on increasing standards. This, coupled with a widespread assumption that the best way to maximise academic success was by selective grouping, led to government guidelines promoting the use of setting. In 1993, all primary schools were encouraged to introduce setting by the Department for Education. This initiative was reinforced in 1997 by the Government White Paper *Excellence in Schools*, which suggested that setting could be beneficial in raising standards. It stated that 'setting should be the norm in secondary schools. In some cases, it is worth considering in primary schools'.

Ofsted also took an interest in the ability-grouping procedures adopted in schools. In the annual report for 1995/6, it was noted that National Curriculum assessment was having a beneficial influence on teaching, leading to a clearer focus on what was to be taught. There was also more precise targeting of groups of pupils, sometimes through teaching groups based on ability (Ofsted, 1997). In 1998, the Chief Inspector's annual report (Ofsted, 1998a) stated that the organisation of pupils into sets was increasing, especially in Years 5 and 6 for maths and English. It was against this background that Ofsted commissioned a survey (Ofsted, 1998b) concerning the prevalence of setting and its effects. The survey found that about 60 per cent of junior schools set for at least one subject in some year groups, while over one third of infant schools and about half of combined infant and junior schools did the same. The higher the number on roll, the more likely the school was to use setting in one or more year groups. It was unusual to find a school of one-form entry or below using setting.

Most schools used setting in Years 5 and 6 only, with the proportion of pupils setted for at least one subject falling steadily the younger the pupils were. Of those schools that adopted setting procedures, 96 per cent set for maths, 69 per cent for English, and 9 per cent for science. Very few schools set for other subjects.

Evidence from inspection confirmed this pattern and showed the use of setting to have increased compared with previous years. In 1997/8, 4 per cent of all lessons observed were setted, compared with 2 per cent in 1996/7. The highest proportion of setted lessons was in Years 5 and 6, where 7 per cent of observed lessons across all subjects were taught in sets. Setting was more likely to be used for mathematics, with almost a quarter of Year 6 lessons taught in sets. In English the proportion of setted lessons was 10 per cent. The pattern of setting at school level also showed a broad match between the two sets of data, with inspection evidence showing that, of the schools that adopted setting, 77 per cent did so for maths, 63 per cent for English and 10 per cent for science. These proportions fell steeply for other subjects, ranging from 7 per cent for information technology to only 2 per cent for history and geography. The research suggested that there was an increasing trend towards adopting structured ability grouping in UK primary schools, with a move away from within-class ability groups in mixed-ability classes which had previously been the dominant form of grouping (Bealing, 1972).

In a more detailed study, which explores the adoption of different types of grouping in the primary school, including setting within and across age groups and within-class ability grouping, Hallam, Ireson, Chaudhury et al. (1999) report that in mathematics, the most commonly set subject, only 24 per cent of schools were adopting same-age setting in Year 6, the year with the highest percentage of setting. This was followed by English (17 per cent) and science (3 per cent). The level of cross-age setting was even lower: 15 per cent in mathematics, 6 per cent in English, with a negligible amount in science. In schools where the majority of classes were mixed age, usually the smaller schools, the proportion was even lower. It is difficult to make direct comparisons from these data to that gathered in the Ofsted study, as the latter provides a less detailed account of the nature of the grouping practices adopted and presents them by type of school (infant, primary and junior). However, the total percentage of schools that reported adopting within- and cross-age setting for mathematics was considerably lower than the 'about half' reported by Ofsted – only 39 per cent in Year 6. While it was clear that primary schools were adopting more setting than previously, it was perhaps not as extensive as the Ofsted data suggested.

The guidance provided for schools relating to the adoption of the National Literacy Strategy also set out the way that pupils should be grouped for the different elements of the literacy hour (DfEE, 1998). While acknowledging the complexity of teaching pupils with different prior knowledge, the guidance stressed that for 75 per cent of the time all the children in the class should be taught together. Differentiation could only be justified in some circumstances: for instance, in classes with more than two year groups or where reception children were taught with Years 1 and 2. Setting was not a recommended option. However, a survey of primary school practices by Hallam, Ireson, Lister *et al.* (unpublished) reveals that schools were interpreting the guidance in very different ways, some reporting that they had abandoned setting and others that they had instituted it in response to the demands of the literacy hour. The changes made depended on previous practice, perceptions of the range of attainment within the class and available resources.

The changes observed over time in the adoption of structured ability grouping in the primary school have been reflected in practices in secondary schools. When selective education was predominant, streaming, banding and setting were commonplace. A 1968 survey (Benn and Simon, 1970) revealed that while some schools (22 per cent) adopted mixed-ability grouping for all or the vast majority of their pupils in Year 7, 70 per cent adopted various forms of banding, streaming or setting.

As comprehensive education spread, there was an increase in mixed-ability grouping (DES, 1978). By 1978, pupils were generally taught in mixed-ability classes in Years 7 and 8, with the exception of mathematics and modern languages, in which setting tended to be introduced earlier (DES, 1978). Only 9 per cent of schools used mixed-ability grouping for the whole curriculum in Year 9, 31 per cent for some of the curriculum. The remaining 60 per cent adopted banding, streaming or setting. By Years 10 and 11, setting for mathematics was the normal practice in 90 per cent of schools (DES, 1978). The most recent survey undertaken, in 1994 (Benn and Chitty, 1996), showed that 50 per cent of schools adopted mixed-ability grouping for all subjects in Year 7. A further 25 per cent adopted mixed-ability practices with setting in no more than two subjects, 9 per cent implemented mixed-ability systems with setting in no more than four subjects and 17 per cent used various forms of setting, streaming or banding in Year 7. By Year 8, setting was adopted by 17 per cent for all subjects, 33 per cent for no more than two, and 24 per cent for not more than four. Twenty-six per cent of schools were using some form of ability grouping. By Year 9 this had increased to 40 per cent. By Year 10 the vast majority of comprehensive schools had abandoned mixed-ability teaching for all subjects (Benn and Chitty, 1996).

Mapping the adoption of structured ability-grouping practices over time, we can see that there was a move towards increased mixed-ability teaching from the 1960s through to the 1980s, particularly for younger pupils, with a gradual reversal of the trend during the 1990s. Much of this has been influenced by political ideology and current educational thought, although the distribution of setting across the curriculum is also heavily influenced by the nature of the subject domain and teachers' attitudes (Reid *et al.*, 1982; Hallam *et al.*, 2001b; Hallam and

Ireson, in press; unpublished, a; b). At primary level there is evidence of considerable within-class, ability and mixed-ability groupings organised by the teacher. This contrasts with secondary school level, where within-class groupings, either ability or mixed ability, are rarely adopted (Slavin, 1987b; Harlen and Malcolm, 1997; Hallam *et al.*, 2001b; Hallam and Ireson, in press; unpublished, a). This suggests that more whole-class tuition and individual work is undertaken in secondary schools than primary.

CONCEPTUAL AND METHODOLOGICAL ISSUES

Which types of pupil grouping are the most effective?

Whether alternative forms of grouping are seen as effective or not depends on the definition of effectiveness adopted and the criteria against which it is assessed. These are rightly the subject of public and political debate. Views of 'effectiveness' change over time in relation to national priorities and for this reason research undertaken in other countries, with different education systems and differing attitudes to and expectations of education, may have limited applicability in the UK.

Without clearly defined guidelines as to what is expected of education, the pursuit of 'effective' practice in schools and research and development work is problematic. While the original version of the National Curriculum did not include educational aims, the most recent formulation (DfEE/QCA, 1999) sets out clearly the values and purposes underpinning education in the UK.

> Education influences and reflects the values of society, and the kind of society we want to be. It is important, therefore, to recognise a broad set of common values and purposes that underpin the school curriculum and the work of schools. Foremost is a belief in education, at home and

at school, as a route to the spiritual, moral, social, cultural, physical and mental development, and thus the well-being, of the individual. Education is also a route to equality of opportunity for all, a healthy and just democracy, a productive economy, and sustainable development. Education should reflect the enduring values that contribute to these ends. These include valuing ourselves, our families and other relationships, the wider groups to which we belong, the diversity in our society and the environment in which we live. Education should also re-affirm our commitment to the virtues of truth, justice, honesty, trust and a sense of duty.

At the same time, education must enable us to respond positively to the opportunities and challenges of the rapidly changing world in which we live and work. In particular, we need to be prepared to engage as individuals, parents, workers and citizens with economic, social and cultural change, including the continued globalisation of the economy and society, with new work and leisure patterns and with the rapid expansion of communication technologies. (The National Curriculum, DfEE/QCA, 1999)

From this are derived two very specific aims:

- to provide opportunities for all pupils to learn and achieve;
- to promote pupils' spiritual, moral, social and cultural development and prepare all pupils for the opportunities, responsibilities and experiences of life.

The inclusive nature of these aims, encompassing academic, personal and social educational outcomes for pupils, sets out a clear agenda for assessing the effectiveness of different types of ability grouping in the UK.

Limitations of the research and methodological issues

Although much research has been undertaken in relation to ability grouping, it is of variable quality, and interpreting the findings can be problematic for a number of reasons. Firstly, pupils can be grouped, by ability, through selective schooling, streaming, banding, setting or within classrooms. Often, different types of grouping operate simultaneously at different levels within the same school (Rutter *et al.*, 1979; van Laarhoven and de Vries, 1987; Slavin, 1987a; Hallam and Toutounji, 1996a; b). American research is often based on students classifying themselves as being in vocational, general or academic tracks, creating further difficulties (Gamoran and Berends, 1987). Even where a school has a policy of mixed-ability grouping, individual teachers may be grouping by ability within their classes. It is therefore difficult for researchers to establish with any clarity the nature of pupil grouping as it is practised within a school (Codling, 1975). The validity of research where comparisons are made between pupils in mixed-ability and streamed, setted or banded groups is therefore called into question.

The second problem concerns the nature of the educational outcomes that are considered. Two major groups of outcomes have been studied, those relating to social and personal development and those relating to academic achievement. There may be a trade-off between these; few research projects have focused on both simultaneously, however. In addition, different studies have adopted different measuring procedures, making comparison across studies difficult.

Academic outcomes have been assessed by a range of different standardised tests, examination performance and course completion. Examinations and courses vary across time, between countries, between different locations within countries and between schools. These are often not comparable. Generally, a narrow range of learning outcomes has been researched with little concern for critical thinking, degree of understanding, creativity and meta-cognitive and transferable skills. Personal and social outcomes have also been assessed in a variety of ways, using different measures of self-esteem, motivation and alienation or interview techniques. Drawing conclusions across studies is therefore problematic.

Thirdly, the research has been limited in its time scale. Very few studies have followed up the long-term effects of selection, streaming, banding and setting on individual personal development and career prospects. Given the current pressures to develop a 'learning society', this is a serious omission.

Fourthly, interpretation of findings is difficult because within any single school, the academic and affective outcomes of grouping are not consistent in size, over time, across subject domains, or between teachers (Newbold, 1977). Teacher behaviour appears to be crucial in mediating the effects of grouping (Barker Lunn, 1970; Newbold, 1977; Gamoran, 1986). There appear to be complex interactions between grouping, teaching methods, teacher attitudes, the pacing of lessons (Burns, 1987) and the ethos of the school (Dar, 1985; Ireson and Hallam, 2001). The grouping of pupils is only one of several factors affecting the learning environment of the classroom; the quality of instruction and the curriculum are central (Creemers, 1994) and both may mediate the effects of pupil grouping (Gamoran, 1986; Passow, 1988). These contextual issues, in particular those relating to the way that grouping is embedded in the ethos of a school and may affect relationships with the wider school community, have largely been ignored. Every school is unique and 'has its own characteristics which are shaped by such factors as its location, pupil intake, size, resources and most important the quality of its staff' (Reid *et al.*, 1987). For this reason, the effects of the same system of pupil grouping may be different between schools and even within the same school as it is implemented differently by individual teachers.

A final problem is that the effects of grouping are not consistent across different groups of pupils. To date, the research suggests that more able pupils benefit from structured ability-grouping procedures while the personal and social outcomes of the less able pupils are adversely affected by streaming, banding or setting. The issue is not merely whether ability grouping is effective, but for whom it is effective, in what ways and whether anyone else suffers as a result.

2
Effects of structured ability grouping on attainment

COMPARISONS OF SCHOOL SYSTEMS

The evidence from research of selective systems of education suggests that they affect opportunity to learn; that is, they deny some students access to aspects of the curriculum. Internationally, variations in opportunity to learn are large and related to the age of selection and the degree of streaming, banding, setting or tracking. Lughart *et al.* (1989) present an overview of studies examining the relationship between opportunity to learn and student achievement. They demonstrate the importance of selective systems in accounting for variation in academic achievement between countries, schools and in the classroom. Scheerens *et al.* (1989) conclude that variations between schools are smaller in countries with comprehensive systems where tracking is absent.

In the UK, a number of studies have compared the academic attainment of pupils in selective and non-selective systems. However, the lack of measures of pupils' prior attainment in much of this research has made interpretation of the findings difficult, although some studies have attempted to compensate by using indicators of social class (Steedman, 1983; Gray et al., 1986). There have also been some difficulties in ensuring that the comparisons made have been between similar populations. Even where comprehensive school performance has been compared with the combined performance of secondary modern and grammar schools, differences between the intakes of secondary modern schools with and without sixth forms (the former having more pupils from families with non-manual occupations) may act as a confounding factor (Kerckhoff et al., 1996).

Overall, the findings have produced mixed results with minimal differences in terms of learning outcomes (Steedman, 1980; 1983; Gray et al., 1983; Marks et al., 1983). Studies in London found that reading scores at age 14 were significantly higher in a grammar school sample and that examination results, measured in terms of 'points' scored for CSE and O levels, were also better. However, this difference was due in part to the fact that selective schools entered more of their pupils for examinations. When the higher entry rates were taken into account, the difference between the two types of school was reduced but not eliminated (Rutter et al., 1979; Maughan and Rutter, 1987). Reynolds et al. (1987) found that the comprehensive system generally fared badly in comparison with selective and secondary modern schools, but as the data focused on boys they argue that it was not truly representative. Research on pupil performance in grammar schools has shown that in some, up to a fifth of pupils do not achieve five GCSE grades A–C (Scheerens et al., 1989).

Marks (1991), comparing figures for O and A level results in Northern Ireland, England and Wales, demonstrated differing patterns of change. In England and Wales in the 1970s, when many schools became comprehensive, there was a plateau, whereas in Northern Ireland, where selection continued, examination results continued to improve. This was interpreted as demonstrating that selective schooling improved examination attainment. However, the explanation may be more complex, relating to the temporary disruption in schools during the process of change in England and Wales. Figures for 1995/6, while indicating high levels of attainment in Protestant grammar schools in Northern Ireland (91 per cent of pupils obtaining five or more GCSEs at grades A–C), showed very low levels (27 per cent) for those attending secondary schools (TES, 1996). Jesson (2000), in research taking account of pupil prior attainment, concluded that none of the evidence presented supported the view that selective 'systems' provided better outcomes than those with fully comprehensive organisation.

Once intake factors have been taken into account, there appears to be little difference between selective and non-selective systems in terms of pupil attainment in national tests and examinations. However, there is some evidence that selective systems may widen the spread of attainment while unselective systems reduce it (Kerckhoff, 1986; Kerckhoff et al., 1996).

WHAT CAN SCHOOL EFFECTIVENESS STUDIES TELL US?

In a review of the literature on school effectiveness studies, commissioned by Ofsted, pupil grouping was not identified as a key characteristic of effective schools (Sammons et al., 1995). However, the organisation of pupils into groups is likely to reflect and impact on nine of the 11 factors which the review outlined as important: shared vision and goals; the learning environment; concentration on teaching and learning; purposeful teaching; high expectations; positive reinforcement; monitoring progress; pupil rights and responsibilities and home-school partnerships. These aspects of school functioning may mediate the effects of pupil grouping.

Levine and Lezotte's (1990) analysis of school effectiveness in the USA included factors relating more directly to school organisation and pupil grouping, and also indicates that pupil grouping is only one of a number of important factors relating to instructional arrangements and their implementation. In contrast, Chubb and Moe (1990), in a study including data from 60,000 pupils, suggested that tracking could account for 30 per cent of the total influence of school organisation on achievement. The extent of this influence could range from one half to two thirds of a year of additional achievement when comparing ineffectively organised schools to effectively organised ones. This reflects the accelerated progress of pupils in higher tracks, facilitated by a changed pace of instruction.

Rutter *et al.* (1979) argue that one important factor in school effectiveness is the balance of intellectually able and less able children in a school. When too many children are unlikely to achieve academic success, an anti-academic or anti-authority peer group culture is more likely to be in evidence. Evidence from the USA, in schools where the catchment area consists predominantly of low income and minority group families, suggests that school populations can become bottom heavy, with smaller academic tracks and larger remedial and vocational tracks (Oakes, 1990). Willms (1986) notes that students of average ability in high-ability schools scored more than a full examination grade higher than comparable students in schools where the majority were pupils of lower ability. Recent research on performance in mathematics (Opdenakker and Van Damme, 2001) suggests that there are important relationships between school composition and school process variables which have important joint effects on achievement independent of initial pupil ability. This has clear implications for selective schooling systems, where 'creaming off' academically able pupils may leave other schools with an inappropriate balance of pupils.

Early research on school effectiveness suggested that schools were equally effective or ineffective for all of their pupils (Rutter *et al.*, 1979; Reynolds, 1982). It has now been demonstrated that schools can differ in their relative effectiveness for different groups of pupils (Aitken and Longford, 1986). Some work suggests that pupils from homes of high socio-economic status (Cuttance, 1992) and of high ability (Gray *et al.*, 1986; Opdenakker and Van Damme, 2001) are more affected by their schools than pupils of lower socio-economic status or lower ability. However, McPherson and Willms (1987), while demonstrating that the effects of comprehensivisation in Scotland varied considerably according to the social class of pupils, found that working-class pupils gained more over time than others.

Schools can be differentially effective for high- or low-ability children (Willms and Cuttance, 1985). Nuttall *et al.* (1989), using multi-level modelling methodology, show large differences in relative effectiveness for different types of pupils in schools in London. Taking the experiences of able and less able children, the differences in performance outcomes could be as small as 11 Verbal Reasoning Quotients or as large as 28, even after adjusting for differences in pupils' abilities at the time of joining the schools. The study found variation in the way in which schools impacted on boys and girls and in their effects on pupils of different ethnic groups, with some schools widening the gap and others narrowing it. Smith and Tomlinson (1989) found similar differences, although the effects were smaller. There are also different patterns of achievement in different subject domains within a school (Levine, 1992) and evidence that departments differ in their levels of effectiveness (Harris, 2000; 2001). Schools can also be effective in relation to different educational outcomes, academic and social (Galloway, 1983; Gray *et al.*, 1983; Steedman, 1980; Mortimore, Sammons, Ecob *et al.*, 1988; Sammons *et al.*, 1997). Taken together, this research suggests that ability grouping in schools is only one of many factors which impact on the academic performance and social and personal development of pupils.

EFFECTS OF WITHIN-SCHOOL GROUPING STRUCTURES ON ACADEMIC ACHIEVEMENT

British studies – secondary level

Relatively few British studies have researched the effects of school type, streaming, banding or setting on academic performance. Early research undertaken by Fogelman and colleagues (Fogelman *et al.*, 1978; Fogelman, 1983) found little difference in performance on standardised tests of achievement in mathematics and reading when ability level was controlled between pupils in different kinds of school. There were differences in examination entry and access to the curriculum, however.

A more recent study by Kerckhoff (1986) compared the reading and mathematical performance of pupils who attended different types of schools and were in different ability groups. He concluded that ability grouping led to a divergence in performance: the performance of pupils in lower ability groups worsened while that of the higher ability groups increased. The pattern was sufficiently clear to enable the identification of differences between a two- and three-group system, the latter producing a greater spread of gain scores.

Findings from small-scale studies have been equivocal. Rudd (1956) found no difference in the attainment of two groups of children, streamed and mixed ability, in the same secondary school. Lacey (1970), researching in a selective grammar school, showed that pupils in the top set received more attention and resources, which led to higher levels of achievement for those pupils but had negative effects on others. A follow-up study after the school introduced mixed-ability grouping showed that the performance of the lower ability pupils improved, although attainment of the most able pupils was unaffected by the change (Lacey, 1974).

There is considerable evidence that increased opportunity to enter for examinations leads to greater pupil success after a change to mixed-ability teaching (Thompson, 1974; Gregson and Quinn, 1978). Research by Newbold (1977) supported the divergence hypothesis in a study of a single comprehensive school which had mixed-ability and streamed halls (houses). Although very similar mean scores were found on a variety of measures of academic achievement, standardised tests of ability, examination performance and teacher-devised tests, there were larger standard deviations in the streamed sample (except in free writing, where there were larger standard deviations in the mixed-ability classes). More differences were found within systems than between them. The low-ability pupils made significant gains in the mixed-ability classes, with no differences observed for the high-ability pupils. A follow-up study (Postlethwaite and Denton, 1978) demonstrated that the less able pupils continued to perform better overall in a mixed-ability situation, without any reduction in the levels of attainment achieved by the more able. Gregory (1984), in a review of the literature, concludes that there have been no consistent findings in relation to the effects of ability grouping on attainment, but that there is an increased risk of lowered teacher expectations for pupils in low sets and streams.

Two recent studies have supported the divergence hypotheses, although the effect has been restricted to mathematics. Ireson *et al.*

(1999; in press) studied change in attainment between Key Stage 2 and Key Stage 3 of the Year 9 cohort in a sample of 45 comprehensive schools adopting different levels of setting. No significant difference in performance in English or science from children in setted or mixed-ability classes was found but, in mathematics, those pupils with higher scores at Key Stage 2 made greater progress in sets, while those with lower scores fell further behind. Wiliam and Bartholomew (2001) reported similar findings between Key Stage 3 and GCSE pupils in six schools. The pupils in the top sets made progress at the expense of those in the lower sets, who slipped further behind. Pupils made most progress in schools where setting was not introduced until Year 10.

These findings suggest that, in mathematics, setting increases existing differences in pupil performance. The subject differences observed in Ireson *et al.*'s study may reflect the greater levels of setting deployed in mathematics classes, the attitudes of teachers of different subjects towards ability grouping and the teaching practices that they adopt (Hallam *et al.*, 2001b; Hallam and Ireson, unpublished, b).

British studies – primary level

When streaming was common practice in UK primary schools, a number of studies were undertaken exploring its effectiveness. Daniels (1961a) found a higher average level of attainment in non-streamed schools, which was accompanied by a gathering of scores around the mean. This appeared to have been caused by an increase in standards of the less able rather than the holding back of the more able. Blandford (1958), in a comparison of streamed and non-streamed schools, found similar results, with a greater spread of scores in streamed schools. Douglas (1964), examining pupils' progress in streamed schools, found little evidence of transfer between streams, with the children in the lower streams making much less progress relative to the top streams.

The most comprehensive study (Barker Lunn, 1970) compared pupils in 36 streamed and 36 non-streamed primary schools on a wide range of criteria. Since many teachers in non-streamed schools practised within-class differentiation, children in these classes were categorised as being 'streamed'. The findings showed no difference in the average academic performance of boys and girls of comparable ability and social class in streamed or non-streamed schools. Being taught by a particular teacher type (pro- or anti-streaming) had no effect on achievement, although divergent thinking, related to creativity, was higher when pupils were taught by non-streaming teachers. This appeared to be related to classroom ethos, which was more permissive than in the streamed classes.

A follow-up study two years later showed no difference in performance at secondary school in relation to prior streaming in primary school (Ferri, 1971). At secondary level no relationship was found between attainment and ability grouping, except that the middle-class children of below-average ability did better in non-streamed schools.

Overall, the early UK research evidence indicates that streaming is no more effective in relation to academic achievement than mixed-ability grouping. Gregory (1984), in a review, described the evidence as equivocal but reported that help with reading, targeted at specific ability levels, could improve achievement (Gregory et al., 1982). There has been little research into recent increases in setting in primary schools and its effect on academic attainment. Self-reports by schools suggest that the effects of setting are mixed (Hallam, Ireson, Lister et al., unpublished). Whitburn (2001), in a study of the progress of over 1,000 pupils at Key Stage 2 in mathematics, found that when the same teaching materials were used, the test results of pupils in mixed-ability classes were significantly better than those taught in sets. Mixed-ability classes were of benefit to the less able pupils, while levels of attainment of the more able did not suffer.

International reviews – primary level

In America there has been intense debate regarding the question of mixed-ability versus tracked school organisation. This has led to a plethora of literature reviews. Of those undertaking major reviews, Slavin's work (1987a; 1990a) tends to support the pro mixed-ability movement, while Kulik and Kulik (1982a; 1982b; 1984; 1987; 1991; Kulik, 1991) support some aspects of tracking. Despite the differences in their conclusions, there is considerable agreement in their analysis of the research findings.

Adopting a best-evidence synthesis, Slavin (1987a) concludes that the evidence for the benefits of tracking for academic achievement at elementary (primary) level is inconclusive. No grouping patterns have been consistently successful. The research reviewed compares ability-grouped classes to heterogeneous classes and uses achievement data from standardised tests or teacher-made tests. It also uses comparable samples either through random assignment or through the use of matching procedures, and studies schools where ability grouping had been in place for at least a semester and involved at least three ability-grouped and three control classes. Slavin concludes that across the 14 studies he reviewed, the effects of ability grouping were essentially nil.

However, a number of studies included in the review demonstrate that where students were regrouped across age levels and given learning materials appropriate for their current level of performance, attainment could be improved in a number of subject areas, e.g. mathematics and reading. Evidence from the success of the Joplin plan, a reading programme which typically allows regrouping across grade-level lines with several age groups working together, supports this. Joplin classes achieved more than controls in 11 of the 14 comparisons made, the median effect sizes for these studies being about +.45. The quality of these studies was high, with two using random assignment and ten using matching. The randomised studies found positive effects on student achievement, as did all but two of the ten matched equivalent studies. The success of the programme could have been due to its novelty value, but Slavin suggested that this was unlikely, as some of the studies demonstrating the largest effects had been in place for three years (Ingram, 1960; Skapsi, 1960; Hart, 1962).

Kulik and Kulik's meta-analysis of cross-age grouping in primary schools (1992) indicates that, when implemented appropriately, it can lead to positive academic effects. They reviewed 14 studies in which children were formed into cross-age groups on the basis of their attainment in a particular subject, typically reading. The overall effects on attainment were positive. The focus on a particular subject area may be important, as a meta-analysis of multi-age classes (Veenman, 1995) found no effects on academic achievement.

Slavin's review also indicates that within-class ability grouping was successful for promoting mathematics achievement in all of the studies and for other aspects of school work in some studies. Meta-analyses of the research on within-class ability grouping supports this (Lou et al., 1996). Overall, Slavin concludes that within-class groupings for mathematics and Joplin or similar programmes for reading were very effective. He could find no support for the overall streaming of children which, he also argues, had the greatest negative social effects.

in some schools where classes include more than one year group. The best known version of this in the USA is the Joplin plan. During reading periods, children in Grades 4, 5 and 6 break into groups covering reading from second- to ninth-grade level. They then return to their classes for a period of reading for enjoyment. Fourteen studies investigated the effects of such cross-grade programmes. Eleven found that they were effective in helping students to learn more. The average effect size in the 14 studies was 0.3; this was small but significant. Two studies reported results separately for ability level. The average effect was 0.12 for the high-ability students, -0.01 for the middle-ability students and 0.29 for the low-ability students.

The review of within-class grouping included 11 studies. Nine reported an overall increase in achievement level where schools used within-class grouping. Only two reported higher overall achievement with mixed-ability instruction. The average overall effect was to raise examination scores by 0.25, a significant but small difference. Successful within-class grouping required the use of different materials for each group.

When classes are enriched for the gifted and talented, the pupils receive richer, more varied educational experiences than would be available to them from the regular curriculum for their age. Such classes are usually characterised by a challenging education programme with distinctive methods and materials. Twenty-five studies were included in the review: 22 found that talented students achieved more. The average affect was 0.41, significantly greater than zero.

Accelerated classes for the gifted and talented provide instruction that allows pupils to proceed more rapidly through their schooling or to finish schooling at an earlier age. Twenty-three studies were included, usually with a moderate level of acceleration, e.g. compressing four years of the curriculum into three, or extending the calendar to speed up progress by using summer sessions. Twenty-three studies used two different study designs. In some, the accelerated groups were compared with their age peers and in others with older highly talented non-accelerates in the grade to which they had moved. Where comparison age groups were the same, the accelerated children did better, with an average effect size of 0.87. Where there were older comparison groups, the effect size was sometimes negative.

Kulik and Kulik (1992) conclude that the differences in curriculum enabled differences in attainment. Multi-level classes, which usually entailed little adjustment of course content for ability groups, typically had no effect on student achievement. Where the curriculum was adjusted, in cross-grade and within-class programmes, there were clear positive effects. Programmes of enrichment or acceleration which involved the greatest degree of curricular change had the largest effects on student learning. The effects of pupil grouping depended on the type of programme. Generally, the higher ability groups benefited, but in these cases there did not appear to be negative effects on the achievement levels of middle and low ability groups.

Overview

Taken together, the evidence from the reviews of Slavin (1987a; 1990a) and Kulik and Kulik (1982a; 1992) indicate that where there are differential effects on achievement related to pupil grouping procedures, they depend mainly on degree of access to the curriculum or, as Carroll (1963) first described it, 'opportunity to learn'. Where pupils are given greater access or opportunity to proceed through the curriculum more quickly, they achieve more. This is supported by UK research, which has observed positive improvement in performance when schools changed to mixed-ability systems and more pupils were entered for a wider range of examinations. Evidence also shows that increased differentiation in performance when setting enables pupils to proceed at different speeds through the curriculum, the higher ability groups making greater progress and the lower ability falling behind. Where pupils are taught in mixed-ability classes, the over-all differentiation of the curriculum is less, and lower-ability pupils tend to perform better (Hallam, Ireson, Mortimore, Hack and Clark, 1999; Hallam et al., 2001b; Hallam and Ireson, unpublished, a; b).

In the UK, the effects of setting may currently be exacerbated by the direct relationship between set placement of the pupil and tiered entry for GCSE, which determines the maximum grade that the child can achieve (Troyna and Siraj-Blatchford, 1993; Boaler, 1997b; Boaler et al., 2000; Gillborn and Youdell, 2000). Pupils are often not aware of the effects of set placement on tiered entry until Year 11 (Boaler et al., 2000; Gillborn and Youdell, 2000). The lack of movement between sets, particularly at Key Stage 4, means that early placement can determine entry level because lower sets may not cover the required course materials (Gillborn and Youdell, 2000). This can cause considerable resentment and lead to those in the lower sets becoming increasingly disaffected (Boaler et al., 2000).

While systems of tiering may be perceived as necessary by examination boards, they limit opportunities for many pupils. More girls are entered for middle tiers than boys (Murphy and Elwood, 1998); African Caribbean pupils are less likely to be entered for the higher tier, as are pupils receiving free school meals. Schools may target pupils who are borderline for getting a C grade, giving them extra tuition and support in an attempt to improve their published performance figures (Gillborn and Youdell, 2000). The necessity for schools to demonstrate improved standards can also lead teachers to enter pupils for 'safe' results, which often means that pupils are entered for a lower tier, restricting their level of success (Gillborn and Youdell, 2000).

The evidence set out above goes some way to explaining why the question of ability grouping is so controversial. Structured ability grouping, of itself, does not appear to lead to consistently better or worse performance in any group of pupils. Pupil performance is related to access to the curriculum and the quality of teaching on offer. In some circumstances, where the curriculum is differentiated, allowing faster progress and more in-depth work, structured ability grouping can be beneficial in raising the attainment of those who are more able. Where the grouping structures lead to low expectations, a reduced curriculum and teaching which is focused on control rather than learning, lower ability groups are likely to do worse.

Neither of these scenarios is inevitable. Teaching in the top sets may be too time pressured and competitive to enable in-depth understanding for some pupils, leading to poor performance. In the bottom sets, teachers with high expectations who have positive relationships with the pupils, engender high levels of motivation and set interesting, challenging work are likely to improve performance. However, as we shall see later, grouping structures themselves have a powerful influence on teachers' attitudes, expectations and pedagogy, and on the way that pupils view themselves and interact with teachers. There is therefore a tendency for structured ability grouping to increase differences in performance between the more and less able. In contrast, in mixed-ability classes, there is less extreme differentiation of the curriculum and pupils' experiences of pedagogy are more similar. This is likely to lead to a reduction in differences in performance between the more and less able, although the quality of the teaching is likely to determine whether there is a levelling up or down. If the work is challenging, stimulating and appropriately differentiated, where necessary, the performance of the high-ability pupils is likely to be maintained and that of the lower-ability pupils raised.

These conclusions leave policy makers with difficult choices. A more palatable approach may be to explore different types of innovative grouping structures which may promote greater attainment for all pupils more consistently. Examples of these will be considered later.

3
Social and personal outcomes of different kinds of grouping

EFFECTS ON PARTICULAR GROUPS OF PUPILS

Historically, the most serious criticisms of selection, streaming and tracking derive from their perceived social consequences. There is clear evidence that the low streams tend to include disproportionate numbers of pupils of low socio-economic status (Douglas, 1964; Oygarden *et al.*, 1971; Sandven, 1971; 1972; Hauge, 1974; Winn and Wilson, 1983; Oakes, 1985; Burgess, 1986; Vanfossen *et al.*, 1987; Peak and Morrison, 1988), some ethnic minorities (Esposito, 1973; Winn and Wilson, 1983; Oakes, 1985; Burgess, 1986; Wright, 1987; Tomlinson, 1987; Commission for Racial Equality, 1992; Troyna and Siraj-Blatchford, 1993; Gillborn and Youdell, 2000), boys, and those born in the summer (Douglas, 1964; Barker Lunn, 1970).

When selective education and streaming was the norm in the UK, it dictated the course of study in all areas. Those in the higher streams and grammar schools were oriented towards university, while those in the lower streams and at secondary modern schools were targeted towards the job market. In Northern Ireland, where selective education continues, figures for 1995/6 show that 91 per cent of grammar school pupils gained five or more GCSE A–C grades, in contrast to only 27 per cent of secondary school pupils. This has clear implications for progression to higher education and subsequent employment prospects.

Even in comprehensive schools, streaming can differentiate between these two paths (Ford, 1969; Burgess, 1983). The structure of stratification in schools, its permanence and relative inflexibility can lead to a marked restriction of future options (Hargreaves, 1967; Lacey, 1970; Ball, 1981; Boaler *et al.*, 2000). In the USA, Oakes (1992) sets out similar arguments in relation to the effects of tracking on the opportunities of low-income, African American and Latino students. College-track students enjoy better prospects for high school completion, college attendance, grades and graduation and, indirectly, high-status occupations than non-college track peers (Vanfossen *et al.*, 1987; Gamoran and Mare, 1989). The College Board in America has also criticised tracking for posing barriers to minorities' access to college (Goodlad, 1989).

In the UK, early studies indicate that the gap in educational attainment between children of different social backgrounds widened as children progressed through school (Douglas *et al.*, 1968; Ross and Simpson, 1971; Fogelman and Goldstein, 1976). Despite the spread of comprehensive education and mixed-ability teaching, the pattern appears to have changed very little. A disproportionate number of pupils from lower-class backgrounds in low-ability sets also find themselves guided into low-status subjects (Tomlinson, 1987; Peak and

Morrison, 1988, Mirza, 1992), as do those from some ethnic minorities (Tomlinson, 1987). There are also gender and ethnic differences. For instance, Asian boys are encouraged to study high-status science subjects in comparison to the low-status more practical subjects offered to Asian girls (Mac an Ghaill, 1988; Smith and Tomlinson, 1989). There appears to be a hierarchy of subjects considered suitable for the less able (Tomlinson, 1987; Smith and Tomlinson, 1989; Gillborn and Youdell, 2000).

EXPECTATIONS

Another perceived negative effect of structured ability grouping highlighted by previous research is its influence on the expectations of pupils regarding their prospects (Gamoran, 1986; Kerckhoff, 1986). Low-stream pupils have low expectations of themselves, a perception which is reinforced by their parents and teachers, leading to self-fulfilling prophecies. Tuckman and Bierman (1971) showed that moving black pupils to a different school and placing them in a different ability group resulted in changed expectations and improved academic progress (cited in Winn and Wilson, 1983). Reuman (1989) also found that early tracking not only shaped expectations of performance but predicted later success because of the system itself. The quality of instruction differed between groups, as did resources. This led to a widening of the gap between groups.

In the USA, students in college tracks are expected to enter college, while others are expected to enter the workforce immediately on leaving school. Students in the lower vocational tracks generally hold lower expectations (Berends, 1995). In the UK, when streaming was commonplace, those in high streams received more encouragement to stay on at school (Hargreaves, 1967; Lacey, 1970). Hallam et al. (2001a) and Hallam, Ireson and Hurley (unpublished, a; b) found that pupils had clear conceptions of the way that their set placement would affect future examination success and ultimately their career prospects.

Gamoran and Berends (1987) argue that because of the symbolic importance of track and stream positions, students and others hold these differential expectations regardless of actual performance or potential. However, not all of the research supports this view. The National Child Development Study showed no differences between streamed and non-streamed schools in their pupils' self-ratings, motivation, or plans for the future (Essen *et al.*, 1978; Fogelman, 1983). Nevertheless, high- and low-set or -track students view the top ability groups as offering a better education and more prestige (Rosenbaum, 1976; Hallam *et al.*, 2001a; Hallam, Ireson and Hurley, unpublished, a; b). In the UK, setting not only affects expectations but sets very real limits on examination entry and possible attainment (Boaler *et al.*, 2000; Ireson and Hallam, 2001; Hallam *et al.*, 2001a; Hallam, Ireson and Hurley, unpublished, a; b).

Parents' expectations are also shaped on the basis of their child's group classification (Reuman, 1989). In the UK, Barker Lunn (1970) surveyed parents' attitudes and revealed that at primary level the classification of pupils was interpreted by parents as an indication of their child's future. Where schools did not stream, the links between the ability of the child and parental aspirations were less close.

EFFECTS ON SOCIAL MIXING

A perceived benefit of mixed-ability grouping has been its promotion of social mixing among pupils. This is a perception which is shared by the pupils themselves (Hallam, Ireson, Davis and Mortimore, 1999b; Hallam *et al.*, 2000; 2001a; Hallam, Ireson and Davies, unpublished; Hallam, Ireson and Hurley, unpublished, a; b). Despite this, a number of studies suggest that at both primary and secondary level pupils tend to choose friends of similar social class, ability and ethnic grouping (Barker Lunn, 1970; Postlethwaite and Denton, 1978; Gamoran and Berends, 1987). In addition, few differences have been found between the friendship patterns of pupils in mixed-ability or streamed classes (Johannesson, 1962; Deitrich, 1964; Neave, 1975).

At primary level, in the UK, Barker Lunn (1970) found that children in streamed and non-streamed schools tended to choose those of similar ability and social class as friends, although a greater number of mixed social class and ability friendships were observed in non-streamed schools. At secondary level, Newbold (1977) suggests that the form unit provided the basis for friendships to develop and that this outweighed any long-standing influence of former primary school associations unless these were linked. The children studied tended to associate with others of similar ability and social class, but this was less marked in mixed-ability forms. Several studies have confirmed that students' friends tended to be in the same stream (Hargreaves, 1967; Lacey, 1970; Rosenbaum, 1976; Ball, 1981; Schwartz, 1981). As the majority of pupils' time at school is spent in the classroom, this is to be expected. The recent adoption of setting procedures, where pupils regroup for different subjects as they progress through school, can split friendship groups and reduce the social support that pupils have developed (Ireson and Hallam, 2001a; Hallam, Ireson, Davis and Mortimore, 1999b; Hallam et al., 2001a; Hallam, Ireson and Davies, unpublished; Hallam, Ireson and Hurley, unpublished, a; b). Some pupils wanting to change set gave as their reason that they wanted to be with friends (Hallam, Ireson, Davis and Mortimore, 1999b; Hallam et al., 2000; 2001a; Hallam, Ireson and Davies, unpublished; Hallam, Ireson and Hurley, unpublished, a; b). Chaplain (1996) found that some pupils reported anxiety when groupings changed and they had to work with different pupils and fit into new structures.

SOCIAL COHESION WITHIN THE CLASSROOM

Closely related to the question of social mixing is the issue of cohesion in the classroom. It has been suggested that mixed-ability teaching can lead to greater social cohesion because pupils help each other and the more able provide encouragement and support for the less able by their example (Findlay and Bryan, 1975; DES, 1978; Reid *et al.*, 1982; Eilam and Finegold, 1992; Scottish Office, 1996). This was certainly a perceived advantage of mixed-ability grouping as perceived by pupils at both primary and secondary level (Hallam, Ireson, Davis and Mortimore, 1999b; Hallam *et al.*, 2000; 2001a; Hallam, Ireson and Davies, unpublished; Hallam, Ireson and Hurley, unpublished, a; b). Primary pupils in particular reported that it was useful to be able to receive help from friends rather than having always to ask the teacher, although some children reported disliking helping others. Peverett (1994), observing the teaching of 9–11 year olds, found little evidence that lower-ability pupils benefited from the presence or support of higher-ability pupils, and studies in the USA have reported that pupils enjoy lessons more when they are grouped with others of similar ability (Kulik and Kulik, 1982a).

There may be differences in the quality of peer interactions in low and high ability groups. Oakes (1982; 1985) found that students in higher ability groups reported behaviour between peers which was more supportive when compared with lower ability classes, where pupils' interactions were often characterised by hostility and anger. Behaviour is often more disruptive in the lower sets (Findlay and Bryan, 1975; Oakes, 1982; Berends, 1995), whereas in mixed-ability classes, lower-ability pupils tend to behave better (Slavin and Karweit, 1985). Slavin and Karweit argue that this is because every class has a norm for appropriate behaviour. Mixed-ability classes are likely to have higher morale and place a higher value on learning than bottom sets, streams or tracks. However, one of the benefits of setting as reported by some secondary pupils is that it reduces disruption of classes by removing those who behave badly (Ireson and Hallam, 2001; Hallam *et al.*, 2001a; Hallam, Ireson and Hurley, unpublished, a; b). Teachers also acknowledge that the allocation of pupils to groups can, in part, be determined by their behaviour (Ireson and Hallam, 2001). Some pupils exhibiting poor behaviour are placed in low groups irrespective of their level of attainment. In other cases, teachers deliberately split up groups of potentially disruptive pupils into different ability groups in order to be better able to control their behaviour. This can lead to group allocation which is totally inappropriate in terms of the child's academic attainment (Hallam, Ireson, Davis and Mortimore, 1999b; Hallam *et al.*, 2000; 2001a; Hallam, Ireson and Davies, unpublished; Hallam, Ireson and Hurley, unpublished, a; b).

SOCIAL COHESION WITHIN THE SCHOOL

The relationship between social cohesion within schools and structured ability grouping is complex. At primary level, early British studies indicated that social adjustment, social attitudes and attitudes to peers of different ability were 'healthier' among children in non-streamed classes (Willig, 1963; Barker Lunn, 1970). Barker Lunn also found more positive attitudes to school and greater participation in school activities among children in non-streamed classes, particularly in those of average or below-average ability. This finding is supported by Jackson's (1964) reports of more co-operative atmospheres in non-streamed schools. Neither school organisation nor teacher type (streaming or non-streaming) had much effect on the social, emotional or attitudinal development of children of above average ability, but they did affect those of average and below-average ability (Barker

Lunn, 1970). The poorest attitudes were found among pupils in non-streamed schools who were taught by teachers who were streamers. Boys of below-average ability had the most favourable relationships with typically non-streaming teachers in non-streamed schools. The more streams, the more negative the attitudes of those in the lower streams and the greater the possibility of them regarding themselves as socially segregated, with the humiliation which this implies (Barker Lunn, 1970). Moreover, children of below-average ability who were taught by typically streaming teachers in non-streamed schools were friendless or neglected by others. Their teachers' emphasis on academic success and dislike of the below average may have been communicated to other pupils who, in turn, rejected the below-average child.

Chaplain (1996) reported similar perceived negative effects on pupils in the lowest groups in secondary schools related to the number of sets. More recent work suggests that where setting is adopted at primary or secondary level, it legitimises the differential treatment of pupils and those in the lower or higher sets can become the targets of teasing (Hallam, Ireson, Davis and Mortimore, 1999b; Hallam *et al.*, 2000; 2001a; Hallam, Ireson and Davies, unpublished; Hallam, Ireson and Hurley, unpublished, a; b). The more that the school highlights the differences between pupils in different groupings, the greater the likelihood that this may occur (Ireson and Hallam, 2001).

At secondary level, the top set was not consistently seen as the 'best' set by all pupils. In about 18 per cent of cases the 'best' set was a high, but not top set. Being in the second set gave status but avoided the label of 'boffin' often attached to those in top sets. There was also perceived to be less pressure in a high but not top set and the opportunity to undertake interesting work but also have fun. A school culture seemed to have developed which was distinct from that of the teachers. It valued the anonymity offered by good but not outstanding performance and denigrated those with the highest and lowest levels of attainment (Hallam *et al.*, 2001a; Hallam, Ireson and Hurley, unpublished, a; b). A smaller-scale study in a single school corroborates this (Hallam and Deathe, in press).

Research in the 1960s and 70s suggested that only those in the lower sets were stigmatised. Although the teasing aimed at those in the top sets appears to be less derogatory in nature, it is a new phenomenon. This may be because of the spread of comprehensive education where pupils of a wider range of abilities attend the same schools or due to changes in society where those holding high-level qualifications do not automatically derive respect for their position or education.

PUPILS' ATTITUDES TOWARDS SCHOOL

The evidence regarding the effects of different kinds of grouping on pupils' attitudes towards school is equivocal. Rudd (1956) found no differences related to ability grouping but reported that streamed children made fewer contributions and paid less attention in lessons. Their behaviour was also more aggressive than that of non-streamed children. An NFER study of 12 schools found greater participation in school life among non-streamed boys but not girls, although the girls were more involved in school teams (Ross *et al.*, 1972). Newbold (1977) found that pupils of early secondary school age were more socially integrated if they were in mixed-ability classes, but that it was only the low-ability children who tended to have a more positive attitude to school life when they were in mixed-ability systems. The differences in attitudes towards school within one system were as great as the differences between systems.

In a follow-up study, Postlethwaite and Denton (1978) showed that pupils in the mixed-ability system had more positive attitudes towards the school as a social community. However, as mentioned on page 39, the National Child Development Study showed no differences between streamed and non-streamed schools in their pupils' self-ratings, motivation, or behaviour at school (Essen *et al.*, 1978; Fogelman, 1983). Similarly, Hargreaves (1967), Lacey (1970) and Ball (1981) found that some pupils were more pro-school than others even within the same stream.

In the USA, Vanfossen *et al.* (1987) noted that students from academic tracks reported fewer disciplinary problems in their schools and were more likely to describe their teachers as patient, respectful, clear in their presentations and enjoying their work. They suggest that these ethos differences may have contributed to differences in achievement and other outcomes and may be related to the proportion of students in the school in academic rather than vocational programmes. However, Hallam and Deathe (in press) found no difference in pupils' views of their teachers depending on their set placement in mathematics.

There is evidence that setting tends to have a detrimental effect on the attitudes towards school of those pupils who find themselves in the low sets (DES, 1989; Devine, 1993; Taylor, 1993; Boaler, 1997a; 1997b; 1997c; Ireson, Hallam and Hurley, 2001; Hallam and Deathe, in press). Pupils in the high sets tend to have more positive relationships with school (Devine, 1993; Ireson, Hallam and Hurley, 2001) although responses tend to be mediated to some extent by relationships with teachers and the perceived quality of the teaching (Hallam and Deathe, in press).

ALIENATION FROM SCHOOL

Much early research on structured ability grouping focuses on the way that streaming or tracking engendered anti-school attitudes and alienation from school. Where whole peer groups felt alienated, anti-school cultures developed. Streaming, it was argued, played a major role in polarising students' attitudes into pro- and anti-school camps (Hargreaves, 1967; Lacey, 1970; Ball, 1981; Schwartz, 1981; Gamoran and Berends, 1987; Abraham, 1989). High-ability pupils in high streams tended to accept the school's demands as the normative definition of behaviour, whereas low-stream students resisted the school's rules and attempted to subvert them. Over time, streaming fostered friendship groups (Hallinan and Sorensen, 1985; Hallinan and Williams, 1989), which contributed to polarised stream-related attitudes, the high-stream pupils tending to be more enthusiastic, those in the low stream more alienated (Oakes *et al.*, 1991). Recent research suggests that this may not have changed. Some groups of students in lower sets are perceived negatively by teachers who find those sets difficult to manage (Bartholomew, 2001). There is also evidence that a substantial minority of pupils do not view the top set as being the 'best', indicating a lack of shared values with teachers in relation to academic attainment (Hallam *et al.*, 2001a; Hallam, Ireson and Hurley, unpublished, a; b). Those in the lower sets also have less positive relationships with school (Ireson and Hallam, 2001; Hallam and Deathe, in press). A major question, as yet unresolved, is whether negative school attitudes result from streaming, setting and tracking or whether grouping procedures merely reflect existing pupil attitudes.

ATTITUDES TOWARDS PARTICULAR SUBJECTS

The evidence relating to ability grouping placement and attitudes towards particular subjects is mixed. Boaler (1997a; 1997b) suggests that some pupils in the top sets for mathematics have negative attitudes, find learning stressful because the pace is too fast, do not have time to develop a deep understanding, and dislike the competitiveness and high expectations, which they find anxiety provoking. Other students, in contrast, find the pace too slow and the competition and high expectations motivating. This indicates that individuals may not respond to structured groupings in the same way. Hallam and Deathe (in press) found that those in the bottom sets had less favourable attitudes towards mathematics than those in the higher sets. However, set placement did not affect pupils' perceptions of their mathematics teachers. Adopting within-class ability grouping seems to lead to more positive attitudes towards the subject being taught (Lou *et al.*, 1996).

ABILITY GROUPING AND ITS IMPACT ON PUPILS' SELF-PERCEPTIONS

The evidence regarding the effects of ability grouping on self-esteem is equivocal. One body of research suggests that placement in the bottom groups has an adverse impact on pupils' self-esteem and self-concept (Lacey, 1974; Oakes, 1985; Gamoran and Berends, 1987). Oakes (1985) argues that for low-track students, self-concept becomes more negative as they progress through school.

Recent UK research supports this. While all aspects of pupil self-concept increased from Year 7 to Year 9 then declined in Year 10, the greatest level of decline was for those in the lowest sets (Hallam and Deathe, in press). Byrne (1988) examined the effect of tracking on adolescents' general and academic self-perceptions and also found significantly lower English, maths and general academic self-concepts among the lower-track students, although there were no significant differences between high- and low-track students' general self-concepts. She suggests that lower-track students placed more importance on their social and physical competencies and valued academic performance less highly. Chapman (1988), reviewing 21 studies, found that decrements were apparent by Grade 3. The negative impact of low attainment on academic facets of the self-concept was greater than the impact on general self-concept.

In contrast, Kulik and Kulik's (1992) meta-analysis found no overall effect of ability grouping on self-esteem. Of the 13 studies included, nine examined the effects of streaming, seven were undertaken in elementary schools and six in junior high schools (middle school or lower secondary school). The overall effect of ability grouping was virtually zero. However, 11 of the 13 studies reported separate effects for high-, average- and low-ability students. They revealed that ability grouping tended to raise the self-esteem scores of lower aptitude students and reduce the self-esteem of higher aptitude students. This suggests that streaming and setting may have a levelling effect on self-esteem, with more able children losing some of their self-assurance when they are placed in classes with children of similar ability.

In part, the mixed findings may be the result of the different measuring instruments used in the research, but may also be due to mediating factors within the school: for instance, ethos, the quality of the teaching and teachers' attitudes towards low- and high-attaining pupils. In addition, self-esteem is not a single entity. General measures of self-concept are only weakly correlated with academic attainment. Self-concept scales which more specifically relate to curriculum areas tend to be more closely related to attainment (Marsh et al., 1985; Marsh and Yeung, 1997). The average level of attainment in the school may also influence self-concept, so that pupils in schools with higher average levels of attainment have lower academic self-concepts than pupils of similar ability in schools with lower average attainment (Marsh, 1991; Marsh and Rowe, 1996).

These effects may be stronger in highly competitive and structured settings where students follow a fixed curriculum and are assessed in comparison with others (Marsh and Peart, 1988). Pupils who participate in programmes for the gifted and talented tend to experience a decline in self-concept, supporting this position (Marsh et al., 1995). Ability grouping provides an immediate working environment where comparisons with others are made within a relatively small attainment span while also providing pupils with hard evidence regarding their place in the academic pecking order as perceived by influential others, i.e. teachers. This is likely to have substantive effects on pupils' self-perceptions in relation to the academic domain where ability grouping is adopted, unless teachers within the school take action to ameliorate the effects.

If ability grouping occurs in a great many subjects, pupils' overall school self-concept is likely to be affected (Ireson, Hallam and Plewis, 2001). Pupils' general self-concept was higher in schools with moderate levels of setting as opposed to schools with high or very low levels. Regardless of the type of ability grouping adopted, pupils who were high achievers at age 11 had higher self-concepts aged 14, as did boys and those from more socially advantaged backgrounds. The degree of setting in mathematics and science had no effect on the corresponding academic self-concepts, although English setting tended to lower the self-concepts of the higher attaining pupils and raise the self-concepts of lower attaining pupils. There were also gender differences in that boys had more positive self-concepts in mathematics and science, the girls in English. Hallam and Deathe (in press) found that mathematics self-concept was best predicted by set placement, perceptions of the mathematics teacher and general self-concept, while school self-concept was best predicted by general self-concept, set placement and negatively by mathematics self-concept. Taken together, the research suggests that complex interactions are in operation which mediate the effects of ability grouping on general, school and subject self-concepts and may lead to different outcomes for low- and high-ability pupils in different schools.

PUPIL EXPERIENCES OF DIFFERENT TYPES OF GROUPING

It is only recently that research has considered pupils' reported experiences of ability grouping. This approach has been exemplified by the work of Boaler (1997a; 1997b; 1997c; Boaler *et al.*, 2000), who researched the experiences of pupils studying mathematics in two contrasting grouping systems, mixed ability and setted. Based on observation of mathematics classes and interviews with students, Boaler outlined the negative consequences faced by students in the schools where setting had been adopted. Eighty-three per cent of the students interviewed in the setted classes wanted either to return to mixed-ability teaching or to change set. This dissatisfaction was not restricted to those in the lower sets. Some of the students in the highest sets (Boaler, 1997b) felt disadvantaged because they found it difficult to cope with the fast pace of the lessons and the pressures of consistently working at a high level. Particularly vulnerable were girls, who wanted to acquire a deep understanding of mathematics but found this impossible in an environment where the pace of work did not allow time for consolidation. While some boys also reported adverse effects of the pressure in the higher sets, they, unlike the girls, tended not to want to move to a lower set (Boaler *et al.*, 2000).

A larger-scale study (Hallam *et al.*, 2001a; Hallam, Ireson and Hurley, unpublished, a; b), using questionnaires supported by interview data, explored the experiences of ability grouping of over 8,000 pupils in 45 schools adopting high or moderate levels of structured ability or mainly mixed-ability grouping. The findings showed that pupils generally accepted the grouping structures operating within their school. Almost two thirds preferred setting to mixed-ability teaching, but this overall trend was overlaid by gender, set placement and socio-economic status factors. Boys, those of low socio-economic status and those in the lowest sets tended to prefer mixed-ability teaching. A significant proportion of pupils were unhappy with their set placement (in mathematics, 38 per cent). Most wanted to change sets in an upward direction to be given harder work and improve their prospects in examinations and their careers and their status within school. A small number of pupils wished to move down a set to improve their understanding and receive work which they perceived to be better suited to their needs. Teachers were important in pupils' desire to move classes – their teaching skills and personal characteristics were both cited. Some pupils indicated wanting to change set to be with friends. There was a tendency for those in the top and bottom sets to experience some stigmatisation as a result of their set placement. However, within these overall trends, there were substantial differences between the experiences of pupils in individual schools (Ireson and Hallam, 2001).

The main reported benefit of structured ability grouping as perceived by the pupils was matching work to their needs. There was also an acknowledgement that setting could take into account prior attainment in different subjects, which streaming and banding could not. There was a perception that where classes were mixed ability, much of the teacher's attention was focused on the less able, but that in such classes pupils could help each other, promoting social inclusion and equality of opportunity. Where structured ability groupings were adopted, they were seen to legitimise and make more transparent differences in pupils' attainment, which was perceived to lead to teasing of high- and low-ability pupils. The negative connotations of the language adopted – 'thick', 'dumb' – were viewed as particularly stigmatising for those of lower ability.

In mathematics, science and English the majority of pupils perceived that the top set was 'best', although 'another high set' was selected by a sizeable minority and a lower set by slightly less. For all subjects status was the single main reason given for a set or class being seen as best, although in English, perhaps because of the nature of the material being taught, the personal qualities of the teacher seemed to take on more importance. There were significant differences in choice of best set between type of school. The top set was seen as best by more pupils in mixed-ability schools.

These findings have been corroborated in a study of pupils' experiences of ability grouping in mathematics across Years 7 to 10 in a single school (Hallam and Deathe, in press). Further, this study demonstrated that low-ability pupils were more frequently called names and that those in the top set believed they were accorded more respect for being in the top set. However, very low mean scores suggested that set placement in mathematics was not an important factor in the evaluation of pupils by their peers.

Some pupils perceived that they were in a lower set because of their behaviour rather than their ability (Hallam *et al.*, 2001a; Hallam, Ireson and Hurley, unpublished, a; b). The evidence suggests that this is more likely to be the case for boys (Tomlinson, 1987; Boaler, 1997b), particularly those of African Caribbean origins (Wright, 1987; Wright *et al.*, 2000). Lack of fluency in English among ethnic minority pupils is often perceived as indicating learning difficulties, which may mean that these pupils are consigned to a lower set than they would have been based on general ability (Troyna and Siraj-Blatchford, 1993; Gillborn and Youdell, 2000).

Awareness of the effects of grouping structures and the rationales for adopting them is not limited to secondary school pupils. Pupils in six case-study primary schools adopting different grouping practices demonstrated understanding and acceptance of the rationale for grouping adopted by their school and were able to outline the advantages and disadvantages of different kinds of grouping as they perceived them (Hallam, Ireson, Davis and Mortimore, 1999b; Hallam *et al.*, 2000; Hallam, Ireson and Davies, unpublished). Where streaming or setting was adopted these structures were perceived as providing work at the right level which would help pupils to achieve their full potential. In one school where mixed-ability teaching was deliberately adopted to encourage the development of social skills and team work, the pupils were able to articulate this aim. In all cases pupils were socialised into the values of the school as established by teachers and accepted by parents. Where structured ability groupings were adopted, as in the case of secondary schools, they legitimised and made more transparent differences in pupils' attainment. Some children, particularly those in the lower groups, experienced teasing and stigmatisation, although in the school where the emphasis was on working together it was the more able pupils who were more likely to be teased. Contrary to popular belief, pupils at primary level were not always aware of the extent of the differences between them. This was particularly true of the boys, who tended to overestimate their ability, especially when they were in mixed-ability classes (Ireson and Hallam, 2001).

THE LONG-TERM EFFECTS OF DIFFERENT FORMS OF GROUPING

Most research has examined the effects of pupil grouping in the short term, although there has been some follow-up of career paths through further/higher education and work. Postlethwaite and Denton (1978) showed that mixed-ability and streamed systems showed few differences in connection with the number and quality of pupils who opted to stay on at school, go on to further education or work. Career aspirations were also similar. Essen *et al.* (1978) found negligible association between school leavers' future plans and their school's ability grouping policy, although aspirations differed according to whether pupils were in the top, middle or lowest range of ability. The proportions choosing each kind of job were broadly similar in spite of different grouping procedures.

Evidence from research considering motivation and training indicates that the long-term effects of negative school experiences include a reluctance to take up training opportunities (McGivney, 1992; Maguire *et al.*, 1993). Pupils' experiences in their school years have a lasting impact on their lives: negative attitudes to learning inculcated during the school years can impact on each individual's motivation to continue or return to education later in life. The values and aims of education espoused within the National Curriculum suggest that attitudes to learning may be an important educational outcome in the 21st century. The way that pupils are grouped within and between schools has effects which go beyond academic attainment (Ireson and Hallam, 2001). Where pupils do not feel valued by the school they will seek other ways of maintaining their self-esteem. This may be through subcultures which hold anti-education values, where it is 'cool' to be disaffected. While schools may be able to 'contain' such behaviour in the short term, in the long term, the alienation of disaffected young people has substantial costs to society as a whole.

4
Teachers, schools and structured ability grouping

TEACHERS' BELIEFS ABOUT ABILITY GROUPING

Early studies of teachers' attitudes towards structured ability grouping in the USA (NEA, 1968; McDermott, 1976; Wilson and Schmidts, 1978), Sweden (Husen and Boalt, 1967), England (Daniels, 1961a; Jackson, 1964; Barker Lunn, 1970) and Israel (Ministry of Education, 1965; Guttman et al., 1972) have revealed generally positive attitudes towards teaching classes where pupils are grouped by ability. Teachers' experience of mixed-ability classes is an important mediator, however (Newbold, 1977; Reid et al., 1982), as are the grouping practices dominant in the school in which they teach (Hallam, Ireson, Mortimore, Hack and Clark, 1999; Hallam et al., 2001b; Hallam and Ireson, in press; unpublished, a; b).

During the 1980s, experienced teachers were found to be more supportive of mixed-ability teaching (Clammer, 1985; Reid *et al.*, 1982), particularly where appropriate resources were available, although as the pressures of external examinations approached teachers tended to prefer ability grouping. However, they often found it more difficult to put into practice than those who had been recently trained to adopt such practices (Reid *et al.*, 1982). Those who were critical of mixed-ability teaching suggested that it failed to motivate and increase the achievement of the highly able, although the less able were perceived to benefit (Newbold, 1977; Reid *et al.*, 1982). The advantages of mixed-ability teaching were seen largely in social terms, while the disadvantage was perceived to be the difficulty of providing appropriate work for pupils of high and low ability in the same class. Recent research has shown that while teachers report sharing materials within their departments to assist with mixed-ability teaching, they still have difficulties relating to a lack of differentiated materials (Hallam, Ireson, Mortimore, Hack and Clark, 1999; Hallam *et al.*, 2001b; Hallam and Ireson, in press; unpublished, a; b).

Reid *et al.* (1982) explored differences in teachers' attitudes towards ability grouping depending on the subject they taught. Where subjects were structured in such a way that learning built on previous knowledge – for example, in mathematics and modern foreign languages – teachers seemed to favour streaming, while the humanities were perceived as particularly suitable for mixed-ability teaching. Ninety per cent of language teachers were sceptical of the possibility of effective mixed-ability teaching. Scientists occupied a middle position, perceiving some difficulties. This may explain the greater number of studies specifically examining the effects of streaming and mixed-ability teaching on achievement, or classroom interaction, in science (Frost, 1978; Plewes, 1979; Harvey, 1981;

Lawrence and Munch, 1984; Hacker and Rowe, 1993). The research, with the exception of that of Frost (1978), found in favour of streamed groups. Those subjects where mixed-ability teaching was perceived as problematic tended to require correct answers and a grasp of abstract concepts.

Recent research (Hallam *et al.*, 2001b; Hallam and Ireson, unpublished, b) supports these findings, demonstrating that teachers' attitudes towards and beliefs about ability grouping were best predicted by the dominant grouping structures in the school where they worked – mixed ability, partially set or set – (standardised beta weight .225) and the subject that they taught (standardised beta weight .078) (Hallam *et al.*, 2001b; Hallam and Ireson, in press; unpublished, a).

At primary level, Barker Lunn (1970) reported that the attitude of the teacher towards mixed-ability teaching was crucial in relation to its implementation in the classroom. Teachers classified as 'typical streamers' were 'knowledge' centred, with an emphasis on the acquisition of knowledge and the attainment of a set of academic standards. They were particularly interested in and concerned for the bright child, concentrated on traditional lessons, gave more emphasis to literacy and numeracy, encouraged competition and approved of selective examinations. Firm discipline was seen as important and the classroom atmosphere was formal.

The typical non-streamer was more child centred, with a greater concern for the all-round development of each pupil. Teaching tended to stress self-development, learning by discovery and practical experience. A more co-operative environment was encouraged, where pupils worked in groups and helped each other. There was also a more permissive classroom atmosphere. These teachers disliked streaming and selective examinations.

PREFERENCES FOR TEACHING PARTICULAR GROUPS

Historically, where ability-grouping structures are in place, teachers have indicated preferences for teaching high ability groups (Hargreaves, 1967; Lacey, 1970; Findlay and Bryan, 1975; Ball, 1981; Finley, 1984), in some cases competing against each other in order to be able to do so (Finley, 1984). This may be because pupils in lower ability classes tend to have more negative attitudes towards school and often exhibit poor behaviour in the classroom, which makes them more difficult to teach (Hargreaves, 1967; Schwartz, 1981; Finley, 1984; Taylor, 1993). Certainly teachers of high ability groups have tended to be more enthusiastic about teaching (Rosenbaum, 1976) and have reported feeling more efficacious (Raudenbush et al., 1992) (although this effect disappeared when the level of pupil engagement was controlled). Perhaps teachers find it difficult to generate interest in learning in pupils in lower ability groups and the resulting lack of engagement undermines their sense of efficacy. Other early research showed that teachers who consistently taught low ability groups tended to become demoralised over a period of time (Hargreaves, 1967; Finley, 1984).

Teachers' attitudes towards teaching low ability groups may have contributed to the alienation of pupils in those groups. Pupils from high ability groups tend to exhibit pro-social behaviour and it is this, rather than their academic achievement, which seems to shape teachers' behaviour towards them (Hargreaves, 1967; Lacey, 1970; Ball, 1981; Finley, 1984; Bartholomew, 2001). Teachers have also been shown to interact with high ability groups more frequently and positively than they do with low ability groups (Sorenson and Hallinan, 1986; Gamoran and Berends, 1987; Harlen and Malcolm, 1997). However, in some schools, presumably where the ethos is supportive of pupils of all abilities, there is some evidence that teachers of low-stream students do view them positively (Burgess, 1983; 1984). In the current UK educational context, where some teachers choose to specialise in teaching those with special educational needs, this may be the case.

ABILITY GROUPING AND PEDAGOGY

Resource allocation

Historically, high ability groups in streamed systems have tended to be taught by those teachers who were perceived as the 'best', usually the more experienced and better qualified. Low streams have tended to be allocated to the less experienced and less well qualified teachers (Jackson, 1964; Barker Lunn, 1970; Ball, 1981; Hargreaves, 1967; Lacey, 1970; Rosenbaum, 1976; Burgess, 1983, Oakes, 1985; Boaler, 1997a; 1997b; Bartholomew, 2001). Some primary schools have perceived this as making best use of teacher expertise (Hallam, Ireson, Davis and Mortimore, 1999a).

Currently, in secondary schools in the UK, allocation of teachers to particular teaching groups tends to be made at departmental level. Heads of department hold different views about how teachers should be allocated, but many decisions are made pragmatically, on the basis of the greatest benefit to pupils. In subjects where there are major teacher shortages, those with relevant high-level qualifications and greater experience are more likely to teach the older students, particularly those taking GCSE or A level courses (Ireson and Hallam, 2001). By default, younger pupils and those in lower ability groups are more likely to have those who are inexperienced and less well qualified.

Teachers working with high ability groups have tended to put more time and energy into their teaching and have spent more time preparing (Rosenbaum, 1976), although in a recent survey this was not reported to be the case (Hallam, Ireson, Mortimore, Hack and Clark,

1999; Hallam *et al.*, 2001b; Hallam and Ireson, in press; unpublished, a; b). They have also tended to be more enthusiastic (Oakes, 1985). Other scarce resources have also tended to be channelled towards high achievers. This contrasts with the current situation in the United Kingdom, where additional resources are available for pupils with statements of Special Educational Need, although some pupils perceive that top sets undertake more interesting activities which in some cases rely on additional resources (Hallam *et al.*, 2001a; Hallam, Ireson and Hurley, unpublished, a; b).

Classroom activities

Where streaming, setting or tracking occurs, the activities undertaken in the classrooms of high-, middle- and low-ability pupils differ considerably. There is often differential access to the curriculum, the top groups benefiting from enhanced opportunities (Ball, 1981; Oakes, 1985; Gamoran, 1990; Boaler, 1997a; 1997b; Hallam, Ireson, Mortimore, Hack and Clark, 1999; Hallam *et al.*, 2001b; Hallam and Ireson, in press; unpublished, a; b). An informal syllabus may also operate where, for the lower streams, topics are omitted and there are different expectations (Ball, 1981; Oakes, 1985; Hallam, Ireson, Mortimore, Hack and Clark, 1999; Hallam *et al.*, 2001b; Hallam and Ireson, in press; unpublished, a; b) The knowledge on offer is generally low status and not suitable for gaining access to higher education (Burgess, 1983; 1984; Keddie, 1971; Oakes, 1985). Studies examining the effects of different types of grouping on gifted pupils have found that it is the use of curriculum materials tailored to their needs which produces the greatest change in attainment (Kulik and Kulik, 1982a; 1987; Feldusen, 1989; Askew and Wiliam, 1995).

A substantial literature now indicates the tendency for instruction in

union in the objectives of teachers in the streamed schools and a tendency for many teachers in non-streamed schools to hold attitudes or implement policies at variance with the stated policy of the school. These factors influenced the development of certain school-related attitudes in the pupils and the motivation to do well in school in children of average and below-average ability. The children in non-streamed schools held more favourable attitudes than pupils in streamed schools; they also participated more in school activities, although in both kinds of school the more able children and those from the higher social classes tended to be more involved.

Recent research at primary level (Hallam, Ireson, Davis and Mortimore, 1999b; Hallam *et al.*, 2000) has indicated that while there may seem to be little difference in school ethos as defined by educational aims included in school documentation or as reported in interviews with teachers, in practice there are substantive differences in the way these aims are operationalised. Overwhelmingly, reported aims in documentation were to enable each child to develop to his or her full potential. Interview data revealed more focus – improving national test scores and raising attainment.

In six case-study schools these aims were pursued through streaming, different levels or types of setting, or mixed-ability teaching, which impacted on the pupils in very different ways, affecting the nature of the teaching, the allocation of teachers to classes, and pupil experiences. Pupils were socialised into the particular practices adopted within each school and generally accepted them, although ethos differences emerged in the level of reported teasing related to ability, the particular pupils targeted and the extent to which pupils were aware of their position in the pecking order. Grouping structures, while they did not define school ethos, clearly played a role in shaping shared attitudes within the school, which in some cases valued some pupils more than others.

At secondary level, Ireson and Hallam (2001) found a tendency, in some schools, to link aims closely to ability-grouping practices, particularly where management views about grouping practices were strongly held. For instance, setting was justified as preparing pupils for life after school, mixed-ability teaching in terms of providing equality of opportunity. In some schools such justification was not in evidence and a more pragmatic approach was adopted.

While there were substantial differences between schools in pupils' attitudes, self-esteem and satisfaction with the school and its grouping practices, these differences did not appear to be linked in any systematic way to the schools' grouping policies, reasons for adopting them, or teachers' satisfaction with them. Pupils generally shared the rationale given by the school for the adoption of particular grouping practices and tended to prefer the kind of grouping that was on offer in their school. The values held by staff were communicated to pupils in everyday interactions: for instance, through unfavourable comparisons made with other groups, reluctance to offer help to particular groups of pupils, or the extent to which homework was set and marked. Pupils learned the degree to which they were valued within the school through these interactions. Where there was a strong shared ethos among the staff which valued academic achievement above all else, this was communicated to pupils, leaving some feeling alienated and others superior. In some cases this was related to the grouping structures adopted, but not always.

Why and how schools adopt particular grouping practices

When considering how to group pupils, schools take account of a range of factors relating to their current circumstances (Hallam, Ireson, Lister *et al.*, unpublished; Ireson and Hallam, 2001). These relate to practical matters of timetabling, staffing, accommodation and resources; making best use of staff expertise; evaluations of pupil learning outcomes; external recommendations, e.g. Ofsted reports; and government guidance (Ireson and Hallam, 2000/1; 2001). The arrival of a new head teacher can pre-empt change (Hallam *et al.*, in press), while parents can also be influential in the practices which schools adopt (Ireson and Hallam, 2001; Hallam *et al.*, in press; Hallam, Ireson, Davis and Mortimore, 1999b; Hallam *et al.*, 2000), particularly in the current competitive climate in which schools find themselves.

At primary and secondary level, school size and the size of the current cohort of pupils are crucial in determining class make-up and, ultimately, practices relating to structured ability grouping (Hallam, Ireson, Lister *et al.*, unpublished; Ireson and Hallam, 2000/1; 2001). The current context of attempting to raise standards has led some schools to target particular groups to enable them to reach national standards (Gillborn and Youdell, 2000). At secondary level, additional considerations may relate to the number of specialist rooms for certain subjects, restrictions on class sizes in specialist rooms, accommodating part-time staff, time for travelling between split sites and co-ordinating the timetable for the sixth form with other schools in a consortium (Ireson and Hallam, 2000/1). Teachers of different specialisms also consider some subjects as more suitable for setting than others (Hallam *et al.*, 2001b; Hallam, Ireson and Davies, unpublished; Hallam, Ireson and Hurley, unpublished, a; b).

Within schools, decisions about the adoption of particular grouping structures are made in different ways. Some decisions are taken by top management and implemented from the top down. Others are made after wide-ranging consultation, some after a proposal from a department. In some cases decision making is devolved to departments. There is a tendency for a more top-down approach to be adopted in schools with high levels of structured grouping (Ireson and

Hallam, 2001). Parental choice of school is also influential. Head teachers often felt they had to introduce structured ability grouping because their intake of able children was decreasing, since parents were sending their offspring to other local schools where ability-grouping practices were already implemented (Ireson and Hallam, 2001).

A further key factor in decisions about grouping at both primary and secondary schools is assessment systems. The introduction of tiers in Key Stage tests and GCSE examinations have led many schools to adopt structured grouping systems to meet examination requirements. At primary level schools have adopted grouping structures to attempt to improve performance on Standard Attainment Tests (Ireson and Hallam, 2001).

Allocation of pupils to ability groups and movement between them

Historically, the evidence suggests that allocation of pupils to streams or sets is a somewhat arbitrary affair and is not based entirely on prior academic achievement or ability (Jackson, 1964; Neave, 1975). Barker Lunn (1970), studying primary schools, showed that 15 per cent of children were in the wrong stream at the end of the school year on the basis of English and arithmetic performance. This percentage was lower in the early primary years and higher in the later years. At the beginning of the next school year, on average a quarter of these children were moved into their correct stream, but three quarters remained in the wrong stream given their test performance. Children remaining in too high a stream tended to improve but those in too low a stream tended to deteriorate. Those in too low a stream were often the younger pupils in the year group and those in too high a stream the older. In the first year of secondary school, Newbold (1977) found vast differences in prior knowledge between intakes from different primary schools. These residual differences remained for at least as long as a year after transfer.

Troman (1988) found that for most pupils there was consensus between test results and teachers' perceptions and judgements, and group allocation was unproblematic. Where this was not the case, teachers tended to rely on their perceptions of pupils, taking into account prior performance, prior performance of siblings, previous grouping allocation and even pupils' physical appearance. Pupils' behaviour or motivation may also be taken into account when set placements are made (Ireson and Hallam, 2001). In some cases, children exhibiting poor behaviour or poor motivation are allocated to lower ability groups but in other instances, schools try to separate disruptive pupils, again leading to inappropriate set placement for some (Ireson and Hallam, 2001).

Recent case studies of primary schools adopting different grouping practices in the UK showed that allocation to ability groups tended to be based on Cognitive Ability Tests, national attainment tests or a combination of both (Hallam *et al.*, in press). Where standardised test scores are used rigorously to allocate pupils to schools or streams, test bias can lead to discrimination against minority groups. Apportioning educational opportunity through performance on standardised tests can also mean allocating very different educational opportunities on the basis of a one-mark difference.

Pallas *et al.* (1994) found that first-grade reading placements did not appear to be based on children's background characteristics; neither were they closely linked to children's academic performance or potential. Ability-group placements resulted from the interaction of individual student characteristics with school organisational processes and constraints. Once children were placed in a group, inequalities in their academic achievement could be heightened over a period of several years (Dreeben and Barr, 1988; Reuman, 1989).

In the USA, students sometimes have some choice regarding the track that they will pursue (academic, general or vocational). Where schools consult pupils about their preferred track, other information is also taken into account. This would appear to overcome some of the difficulties outlined above; however, pupils' views of themselves are inevitably influenced by others' attitudes. Qualitative studies suggest that race and social class influence secondary-school placement over and above achievement because students from different backgrounds receive different information, advice and attention from counsellors and teachers (Cicourel and Kitsuse, 1963; Oakes *et al.*, 1992). Parents also lobby schools to get their children higher school placements (Oakes *et al.*, 1992; Useem, 1990).

Although in theory movement between streams, bands or sets is possible, in practice it is restricted (Barker Lunn, 1970; Douglas, 1964; Dentzer and Wheelock, 1990; Peak and Morrison, 1988; Rist, 1970; Devine, 1993; Taylor, 1993; Troyna, 1992; Commission for Racial Equality, 1992; Gillborn and Youdell, 2000). The importance of students being able to move sets has been stressed for the successful operation of structured grouping systems (Ofsted, 1998b), but the evidence suggests that in practice there is very little movement. This is often the case even when teachers are aware that pupils are wrongly allocated (Barker Lunn, 1970; Troyna, 1992). One problem is that there is often a gap between work that has been undertaken and requirements for the higher set (Jackson, 1964; Ireson and Hallam, 2001). Where subjects are taught on a carousel basis there may be timetabling difficulties. A further problem is that in order to move some pupils to a higher set others have to move down (Ireson and Hallam, 2001). Where children do change stream in an upward direction, they tend to do better; when they move in a downward direction, they tend to do worse (Barker Lunn, 1970).

5
Alternatives to structured ability grouping and solutions for the future

MIXED-ABILITY TEACHING

When the 1960s shift in educational values towards equal opportunities occurred, streaming declined and mixed-ability teaching became the most common form of grouping in primary schools (Lee and Croll, 1995). It also became more popular in the lower years of secondary education. Its advocacy in the Plowden Report (1967) and concerns about disaffection and alienation at secondary level (Hargreaves, 1967) assured its increasing implementation through the 1970s.

The Plowden Report indicated that mixed-ability teaching would provide all pupils with equal access to a common curriculum and would promote the matching of individual learning programmes to the needs of individual pupils (DES, 1978). In these terms, the success of mixed-ability teaching depended on the teacher moving away from whole-class teaching to being able to cater for the full ability range of the class through individualised learning programmes (Gregory, 1986). The Plowden Report recognised that it would be difficult to translate this ideal into practice.

In fact, in most cases, the ideal was not translated into practice (HMI, 1978; Kerry and Sands, 1984). Observation of teachers in the classroom has shown that teachers tend to teach at a whole-class level to an 'imaginary average' child, even though the range of ability necessitates differentiation within the class (HMI, 1978; Wragg, 1984; Hacker and Rowe, 1993). The style of teaching adopted has been similar to that adopted in set or streamed classes (Rosenbaum, 1976; Barr and Dreeben, 1977; Rowan and Miracle, 1983; Boaler, 1997a; 1997b). Whole-class teaching has predominated and there has been little evidence of genuine mixed-ability group work. Teachers at primary level have often seated pupils by ability, but pupils have worked individually. Able pupils have sometimes acted as teachers' aides to help the slower learners.

Group work has tended to be used as an organisational device (Galton et al., 1980); group composition has often been based on decisions about classroom management, and much group work has been described as limited and impoverished, time being spent undertaking trivial tasks (HMI, 1978; 1979; Sands, 1981a; 1981b; Reid et al., 1982). The cognitive demands made on students have tended to be low, as have the quality of the verbal interactions between pupils (Kerry, 1982b; 1982c; Sands and Kerry, 1982; Kerry and Sands, 1984). Few group tasks have made sufficient cognitive demands on the more able, and in many cases have not stretched average pupils. Few teachers have adopted individualised learning programmes to satisfy the needs of their pupils (Kerry, 1982a; Kerry and Sands, 1984), except where work cards or textbooks are used, often in mathematics, or where reading schemes exist.

Overall, little differentiation has occurred. This has led to higher-ability children being insufficiently stretched (HMI, 1978; Wragg, 1984; DES, 1992) and some lower-ability children being unable to cope with the work. The evidence indicates that this also applies to streamed and set classes (DES, 1992). Generally, pupils' needs have not been met by mixed-ability teaching, as it has been practised, at either primary or secondary level (DES, 1991; Ofsted, 1993; 1994; 1995).

Even teachers considered able to deal with mixed-ability classes effectively have experienced problems providing instruction at appropriate levels for high- and low-ability pupils (DES, 1991; 1992; Ofsted, 1994). Both groups have tended to become bored, although for different reasons. In the case of low-ability pupils, it has frequently led to disruption (Kerry, 1982a). Teachers have tended to make inadequate use of assessment information and often lack detailed knowledge of the range of ability in their classes. Some have been reported as insufficiently skilled in recognising the particular needs of boys and girls, of children from ethnic minority groups or more able pupils. There has also been a tendency for teachers' expectations of pupils to be too low, particularly in inner-city schools (Ofsted, 1993).

Successful mixed-ability teaching relies heavily on teacher skills (Reid *et al.*, 1982). Teachers need to be flexible, use a variety of teaching modes in one lesson, vary the pace and style of approach, use a range of audio-visual media and encourage a variety of pupil activities. They have informal relationships with their pupils, involve pupils in decision making and engage them in learning activities (Kerry and Sands, 1984).

To successfully teach mixed-ability classes, teachers need access to appropriate resources and facilities (Schools Council, 1977; Ingleson, 1982), and one difficulty is that they have often had to spend a great deal of time developing differentiated materials for teaching in mixed-ability classes. There are also strong arguments that mixed-ability teaching may be better suited to some curriculum areas than others (Kerry, 1980b; Reid et al., 1982; Hallam et al., 2001b; Hallam and Ireson, unpublished, a; b). While teachers acknowledge that teaching ability-grouped classes is easier, they strongly agree that learning how to teach mixed-ability classes is extremely beneficial for developing teaching skills (Hallam, Ireson, Mortimore, Hack and Clark, 1999; Hallam and Ireson, in press; unpublished, a).

WITHIN-CLASS GROUPING

Within-class grouping of various types has been adopted in primary schools in the UK over a number of years (Harlen and Malcolm, 1997), but it has usually been on a rather informal basis (Hallam and Toutounji, 1996a; b). At secondary level, there is little evidence of its use (Hallam, Ireson, Mortimore, Hack and Clark, 1999; Hallam et al., 2001b; Hallam and Ireson, unpublished, a; b), while at primary level teachers tend to use grouping as a means of organisation rather than to promote particular learning activities.

Evidence from international literature suggests that there can be positive academic and social effects for all pupils when within-class grouping procedures are implemented appropriately (Creemers, 1994). Within-class grouping provides teachers with the opportunity to meet the needs of pupils of different abilities while reducing the problems inherent in managing individualised learning. Pupils can learn to support each other while working in groups, and working cooperatively may increase pupil motivation. Where pupils help each other pressure on the teacher may be reduced. Pupils also have the opportunity to develop their social and communication skills. Within-class grouping can be based on a range of different pupil attributes, of which ability may be one.

International research reviews of within-class grouping procedures suggest that there are positive academic effects for all pupils when within-class grouping procedures are implemented appropriately (Bossert, 1988; Johnson and Johnson, 1990; Slavin, 1990b; Topping, 1992; Cohen, 1994; Creemers, 1994). In the UK, the need for a greater emphasis on group work within the classroom has been stressed frequently. This may be in ability groups, to assist in the acquisition of basic skills through increasing interaction between teachers and pupils (DES, 1978; Barker Lunn, 1984; Mortimore, Sammons, Stoll et al., 1988), or in mixed-ability groups, to facilitate particular tasks. Earlier reviews considering UK research have been undertaken by Yeomans (1983), Bennett (1985), Galton and Williamson (1992) and Harwood (1995).

The largest UK project on within-class grouping (Galton et al., 1980) identified several different kinds of group work: joint group work, where pupils engage in specific tasks which contribute to an overall theme; seated group work, where children sit together but work individually, albeit undertaking the same work; and co-operative group work, where ideas are pooled as part of a joint piece of work. Observation revealed that 80 per cent of group work was seated group work (Galton et al., 1980; Galton et al., 1987). Joint group work could be found in most classrooms (Galton, 1981) and was generally used in art, craft, and general studies but not in relation to basic skills. Little collaborative work was observed.

Other UK research has explored the kinds of interaction which occurs between pupils when they are working on particular tasks in groups. Taken together, the evidence from this and international research suggests that:

- When pupils work in groups on specific tasks, self-esteem and motivation can be enhanced (Slavin, 1990b; Galton and Williamson, 1992).
- Groups function best when they are mixed ability, including the most and least able. High-ability pupils make a key contribution to group functioning and also enhance their own skills (Swing and Peterson, 1982; Bennett and Cass, 1989; Webb, 1991).
- Groups should, where possible, be representative in terms of gender and ethnic groupings (Slavin, 1990b).
- Teachers need to encourage groups to work independently and intervene rarely so that decisions are reached by the group (Harwood, 1989; Slavin, 1990b; Cohen, 1994).
- Group work is valuable for the development of exploratory talk (Barnes et al., 1969; Barnes and Todd, 1977; Tough, 1977).
- Success in group tasks depends on pupils' ability to raise questions, to listen attentively to each other, and to manage disputes whenever they arise (Tann, 1981).
- Group processes and performance differ depending on the nature of the task (Tann, 1981; Biott, 1987; Bennett and Dunne, 1989; Cohen, 1994).
- Levels of interaction are higher when the task is practical (Bennett, 1985).
- When the task involves discussion of abstract ideas, the level of interaction may be low but of a high quality. Teachers should not be discouraged by this (Dunne and Bennett, 1990; Galton and Williamson, 1992).
- Problem-solving tasks with a clear measurable outcome tend to

generate a higher level of collaboration than open-ended tasks (Crozier and Kleinberg, 1987).

- Pupils need to be taught how to collaborate. This involves the teacher setting clear goals and giving immediate feedback on progress through discussion (Webb, 1983; 1985; Glaye, 1986; Biott, 1987; Burden *et al.*, 1988).

In the UK, most within-class grouping practices are carried out by teachers working to their own rationale. They have received little guidance as to the most effective ways to group pupils (Ireson and Hallam, 2001). This is clearly a serious omission.

PRACTICAL SOLUTIONS FOR THE FUTURE

Taken together, the evidence reviewed above suggests that the major factor in the effectiveness of pupil grouping (in terms of raising attainment and maximising positive personal and social development) is that it offers sufficient flexibility to meet changing demands at school, class, group and individual levels. Highly structured school-based systems tend to lack this flexibility. The most appropriate ways for individual schools to develop flexibility in grouping depends on their size, resources and pupil intake. There is no simple 'off-the-shelf' recipe for success. Pupil needs are likely to change over time and schools must be able to respond to them. In addition, where there is a perceived need for change, implementation must take account of existing staff attitudes and allow time for discussion of different options so that staff have ownership of new systems.

A major consideration is the age of the pupils and how the grouping system can not only ensure their attainment academically but promote positive social and personal development. In primary schools, systems which require a large measure of independent, unsupervised work and give pupils a high degree of choice may be inappropriate. As pupils progress through secondary school, however, where there are currently high levels of disaffection, motivation can be increased by offering pupils choice and giving them much greater responsibility for their own learning. This type of system also offers preparation for lifelong learning in that it enhances the development of transferable learning skills.

Whatever systems are adopted, they should be carefully considered before implementation and their effectiveness monitored over time, taking account of the wide range of factors identified earlier. This information can be used to refine policy and practice or, if necessary, provide the impetus for major change. Efforts to make grouping practices more effective need to be regarded as an ongoing long-term commitment. There are no quick-fix solutions.

Setting

One option for schools is to adopt structured grouping systems, such as banding or setting, but attempt to minimise their negative effects. In practice this would mean that:

- Students should remain in mixed-ability classes for the greater part of the time, their main point of identification being with a mixed-ability class.
- Structured ability grouping should be adopted only where teaching and learning in the subject domain depend on pupils having shared prior knowledge and levels of attainment.
- Procedures for assigning pupils to sets should be based on attainment in that particular subject, not general achievement or

other factors (for example, behaviour).

- To reduce stigmatisation, schools should enable greater flexibility of movement between groups and reduce the extent of differentiation between sets. Parallel groupings should be adopted, e.g. five parallel sets rather than ten differentiated sets.
- Progress should be assessed frequently, followed by reassignment to different groups where appropriate.
- Where necessary, 'bridging' groups should be set up to enable pupils to cover work needed for moving to a higher group.
- Within groups, teachers must vary their pace and level of instruction to correspond to students' needs, adopting a range of methods and resources.
- Some differentiation of work should occur within the class.
- High-status teachers should be allocated to teach the lower sets.
- Teachers should have high expectations of pupils in the lower sets.
- Pupils should not be denied access to the curriculum or opportunity to take examinations because of their group placement.
- The school should provide those pupils who are less academically able with opportunities to excel in other areas.
- The school should demonstrate that it values all of its pupils.

The particular benefit of setting is that it allows work to be set at an appropriate level for the pupil and makes the management of learning easier for the teacher. If the drawbacks can be minimised as outlined above then it may be an effective grouping practice. The danger for schools is the development of an ethos which stresses academic achievement to the exclusion of all else and an environment where high ability is reified, leaving the majority of pupils feeling unvalued with a subsequent loss to their self-esteem, confidence and academic attainment.

Vertical grouping

A large proportion of small primary schools, of necessity, have to adopt vertical grouping structures: that is, putting children in classes which include more than one year group (Bouri and Barker Lunn, 1969; Draisey, 1985; Arrowsmith, 1989; Veenman, 1995; Hallam, Ireson, Chaudhury et al., 1999). Vertical grouping has been adopted by some schools because of the social and family-like structure of classes where pupils, at least one year apart in age, are taught together by the same teacher for several years. The purported benefits are not dissimilar to those of mixed-ability teaching (Veenman, 1995):

- Pupils have the opportunity to form relationships with a wider variety of children.
- A wide diversity of pupils demands that teaching is individualised.
- The complex and changing social environment in such classes encourages the development of a balanced personality.
- The self-concepts of the less able older children are enhanced when they are asked to help younger students.
- The student stays with the same teacher for several years, allowing closer and more secure relationships to develop.
- Fewer anxieties about learning develop because the atmosphere is conducive to academic and social growth.
- Younger students can benefit from the opportunity to observe, emulate and imitate a wide range of behaviour exhibited by older students, while older students have the opportunity to take

responsibility for younger students.

- Vertical grouping promotes co-operation and other forms of pro-social behaviour and minimises competition and the need for discipline.
- The use of different learning materials provides opportunities for younger students to benefit from exposure to more advanced curricula while providing older students with the opportunity to benefit from reviewing earlier work.
- Students at different levels of cognitive development can provide intellectual stimulation for each other.
- Vertical grouping enables a relaxation of the rigid curriculum with its age-graded expectations, which are not appropriate for all pupils.

Reviews of the effects of vertical grouping (Pratt, 1986; Miller, 1990; Veenman, 1995) conclude that there are no significant differences between cross-age and single-age groupings on pupils' academic achievement or social and personal development. However, teachers' feelings are generally negative. They find that it increases their workload, that the management of the class is more difficult because they perceive that they are trying to teach two classes simultaneously, there is less opportunity for oral instruction because teaching one group may disrupt the other, there are more interruptions in the learning process, pupils receive less individual attention, and it is harder for pupils to concentrate on their work. Teachers also comment that they have not received training for vertical grouping (Veenman, 1995). As we saw earlier, cross-age or vertical grouping practices have been adopted in the US, targeted at particular areas of learning, e.g. literacy. The evidence suggests that this can be successful (Gutierrez and Slavin, 1992).

Structured gender groupings

Some schools, in attempting to optimise their pupils' performance, have explored whether teaching girls and boys separately might be beneficial in some curriculum areas. While, overall, there has been insufficient large-scale research to demonstrate whether separate teaching of boys and girls is beneficial to either in the short or long term, some documented case studies illustrate possible practice. For instance, one school adopted single-gender classes in Year 9 for the teaching of English to match gendered learning styles to teaching (Ireson, 1998). In classes for boys the learning environment was competitive, progress to the next level was clear, the pace was quick, the delivery punchy, activities were set and undertaken in short bursts, instructions contained specific information about what was required and when, feedback was specific and related to national examination levels, much work was oral, and there was little written work. The teacher stressed short- and long-term goals and focused on concrete learning outcomes; there was much praise and encouragement. The boys reported that the single-sex classes enabled them to work without distraction and the need to impress the girls. They also felt more able to ask the teacher for help. Teachers reported that the boys spent more time on tasks, were better able to think about their learning, developed considerable meta-cognitive skills, were better motivated, and had improved self-esteem. A team spirit also developed within the class.

In the girls' class, the teacher reported difficulties in getting the girls to contribute to discussions, although they enjoyed undertaking written work, which was of a very high standard. The pace of the lessons was faster than previously with no interruptions, no risk of indiscipline and work which was very focused. No evidence about attainment was available.

Modularisation of the curriculum

Groups can be structured through the modularisation of the curriculum. This allows students greater choice and control over the way in which they progress through school. Such a system, fully adopted at secondary level, could facilitate the broadening of access to learning throughout the community. Long-term developments might include classes taking place in the evenings and at weekends in addition to 'normal' school times. Timetabling would become more flexible and there would be more stress on independent study, with an increase in library and computer facilities to make this possible. Schools would become centres of learning for the whole community, with classes including adults and school-aged children. Such a scenario would enable schools to play a central role in the development of a learning society. Such developments are likely in the long term as educational structures change in response to changing patterns of employment.

Currently, all-embracing modular systems have not been implemented in the UK within the compulsory phases of education, although beyond it they have flourished for many years. However, some schools have developed systems which are semi-modular and operate alongside the National Curriculum. For instance, in one such school a modular curriculum was introduced alongside the core curriculum in Year 9 for 16 per cent of the time, increasing to 28 per cent of the time in Years 10 and 11 (for details see Ireson, 1998). The purpose was to raise standards through improving student motivation by promoting personal ownership of learning, offering as wide a range of subjects as possible, allowing students to decide how much time they wanted to commit to particular subjects and giving them the opportunity for some specialisation. Overall, the modular system had positive benefits. It operated in a market so that staff had to make the modules attractive to students and were constantly challenged to make them interesting and develop new ideas. Because pupils taking core and optional modules were taught together, in groups of different sizes, mixed ability and mixed age, teachers had to adopt a range of teaching methods and be flexible. Students were able to make choices, plan their own learning and were asked to evaluate each module, giving them a sense of involvement which improved motivation, reduced disaffection and promoted positive self-esteem. The flexibility of the modular system enabled a range of examination choices to be made and helped pupils to consolidate work by taking modules which supported their core areas. The disadvantages included the complexity of the administration, difficulties in monitoring pupils' routes through the modules, the need for each module to be self-contained, the modules currently being at only one level, the expense in staffing terms, and pupils tending to make stereotypical choices. However, the impact on academic achievement and the social and personal development of the pupils was considerable (Ireson, 1998).

The main benefits of modular systems lie in the way that they can empower learners and increase motivation and self-determination. They also offer flexibility. Learners can select modules which will satisfy their needs and the curriculum can be differentiated through successful completion of some modules being prerequisite to the taking of others. Modularisation can facilitate the integration of academic and vocational pathways and may be the simplest way to reduce disaffection and improve attendance at school.

Special activity groups

Children in the UK have traditionally been withdrawn from classes in order to provide them with additional support in specific areas, often literacy. However, 'special activities' are provided for groups formed across or within year groups or within classes for a very wide range of purposes. Activity groups can be set up to satisfy particular short-term needs for particular groups of pupils: for example, intensive literacy courses. Facilities might be available on a permanent basis, with pupils slotting in and out as required – for instance, in units to support pupils at risk of exclusion (Hallam and Castle, 1999). Alternatively, time might be allocated each week within the timetable to offer a range of special activities: for example, study skills classes (Selmes, 1987), thinking skills classes (McGuiness, 1999), extension or catch-up work, or social skills classes (Hallam, 1996). There are many possibilities. Specific groups can be run alongside normal curriculum classes to offer integrated provision for pupils with moderate to severe learning difficulties (Ireson, 1998). Groups may also be run outside school hours to support student learning or develop further skills (Sharp et al., 1999). The main advantage of groups set up for special activities is their flexibility. Whether they are set up to withdraw pupils from curriculum subjects or tutor group time, are on offer in the lunch hour or after school, or are timetabled as special activities, they offer flexibility which other methods of structuring groupings do not. They can be offered for short periods of time to satisfy particular needs without disruption to the whole school timetable.

Co-operative learning

Co-operative learning techniques can be applied in several ways. All methods involve pupils working together to learn and taking responsibility for one another's learning as well as their own. There are three fundamental principles: rewards are given to teams; each individual is accountable for their own contribution; and each team member must have an equal opportunity of being successful. For example, in Student Teams-Achievement Divisions (STAD), pupils are assigned to four member learning teams mixed in prior levels of knowledge, gender and ethnicity. The teacher presents the material to be learned. The pupils then work in teams to ensure that they have all mastered the lesson. Pupils are then tested on the material to be learned. At this point they must work independently. Scores are compared to past team averages and points are awarded on the degree to which past performance is matched or exceeded. The points are summed to derive team scores and from this team's meeting certain criteria may earn further rewards. The whole process is undertaken over a number of lessons. Such techniques have been adopted with learners of all ages from seven to college entrance. They are most appropriate for areas with well-defined learning objectives. A variant replaces the tests with competitions, which provide an added incentive for the children.

Another alternative is called Team Assisted Individualisation. This combines co-operative learning with individualised instruction and was designed to be used in mathematics lessons. Teams comprise four members of different ability and with different prior knowledge. The pupils enter an individualised sequence of work based on a test of their prior knowledge on that topic. They then proceed to work at their own pace. Team members check each others' work and help each other with problems. Final unit tests are taken without help and are marked by pupil monitors. Each week the teacher totals the units acquired by each team. Rewards are then given for team performance. The teacher's time in class is spent on explaining new topics to small groups of children drawn from the various teams who are working on the same topic or level, so that although the teams are mixed ability, the teacher works with pupils of the same ability.

If the procedures are undertaken appropriately, co-operative grouping can be a very effective way of supporting academic learning and can also have positive social effects (Slavin, 1990b). Learning outcomes vary according to the quality of the method used and how well it is implemented. Two things are important for success: group goals and individual accountability. When these are both present, the results are consistently positive. In addition, co-operative learning rarely has negative effects and does not hold back able pupils. Where co-operative learning is adopted, children express greater liking for their classmates. It promotes ethnic mixing and inter-ability friendships and improves attitudes to school. It also increases self-esteem, has positive effects on achievement for all children, and improves the integration of children with special educational needs (Slavin, 1990b). Although Bennett (1985) has outlined methodological difficulties in the evaluative research undertaken in the USA, implementation of co-operative grouping procedures in Holland, where there are certain cultural similarities with the United Kingdom (Roeders, 1989), have shown positive academic and social outcomes. Where it is unsuccessful it is often because the procedures have been inappropriately applied, teachers failing to carry out the necessary testing, recording of progress and feedback procedures.

In the USA teachers have found the methods easy to use and pupils seem to like them. They provide an appropriate means of structuring and managing within-class groups, particularly in primary schools and the lower secondary years. Such groupings provide pupils with structured opportunities to learn from each other while demonstrating a degree of independence from the teacher. At all levels where they have been deployed they have been demonstrated to be effective (Cohen, 1994; Creemers, 1994).

Mastery learning

Mastery learning (Bloom, 1976) involves the teacher introducing a topic which has clearly identifiable criteria for attainment. Pupils spend time learning and working on relevant materials and are then tested. Those students who do not achieve mastery, which is usually set at 80 per cent or 90 per cent accuracy, are given feedback and corrective activities by the teacher or pupils who were successful on the test, and the topic is explained again using alternative methods and materials. Those pupils who initially failed the test retake it. When a specified number of pupils have mastered the topic (usually 80 per cent) the class move on to another topic. In some cases this cycle may be repeated more than once to ensure a higher level of mastery.

Reviews of mastery learning (Lysakowski and Walberg, 1982; Bloom, 1984a; 1984b; Walberg, 1984; Guskey and Gates, 1985; Kulik and Kulik, 1986; Kulik and Kulik, 1990) consistently show that mastery learning groups in no case perform worse than controls and often do better. Where mastery learning procedures have been adopted in the UK they have had promising results (for example, Parkinson *et al.*, 1983; Arblaster *et al.*, 1991). Slavin (1987c), while criticising aspects of mastery learning, believes that it has considerable potential, although its structure has tended to restrict its use to tasks that have very clear and measurable learning outcomes. Although there are practical difficulties for the teacher in the management of the time when some pupils have completed the work and others have not, it can be an extremely useful technique to ensure that everyone has grasped the essentials of a particular topic.

There are also personalised systems of mastery learning, notably the Personalised System of Instruction or the Keller Plan (Keller, 1968), used in higher education in the US. This involves establishing unit objectives for a course of study and developing tests for each unit. Students choose when to take a test and may resit it as often as they wish until they achieve a passing score. Students typically work on self-instructional materials and/or with peers to master the course content. Lectures are given to supplement rather than guide the learning process. The system is extremely effective in raising standards, with a very high proportion of students achieving the highest grades.

Mixed-ability teaching

Despite the difficulties with mixed-ability teaching outlined earlier, it has some advantages. The evidence suggests that mixed-ability teaching:

- can provide a means of offering equal opportunities
- can address the negative social consequences of structured ability grouping by encouraging co-operative behaviour and social integration
- can provide positive role models for less able pupils
- can promote good relations between pupils
- can enhance pupil/teacher interactions
- can reduce some of the competition engendered by structured grouping
- can allow pupils to work at their own pace
- can provide a sense of continuity and security for primary pupils when they transfer to secondary school
- forces teachers to acknowledge that the pupils in their class are not a homogeneous group
- encourages teachers to identify pupil needs and match learning tasks to them.

For mixed-ability teaching to be successful, teachers need to be highly skilled and supported by a wide range of resources differentiated to satisfy pupil needs across the ability range.

Within-class ability grouping

United Kingdom research on group work has indicated that collaborative group work is more effective when it is carried out with mixed-ability groups. However, there may be circumstances where teachers wish to group pupils within the class by ability for instructional purposes and the setting of work. When they do this they need to take decisions about the size of the groups. This will inevitably influence their homogeneity.

The size of groups may depend on a range of factors which are out of the teacher's control: for example, classroom size and the arrangement of the furniture (Harlen and Malcolm, 1997). The evidence suggests that within-class ability grouping is most effective when it occurs with pupils in groups of three or four (Lou et al., 1996), although groupings of such small numbers will inevitably reduce the amount of time that a teacher can spend with any particular group. The evidence also indicates that such groups are most productive when they work together over a number of weeks (Lou et al., 1996).

The main advantage of adopting grouping structures within as opposed to between classes is their flexibility. Pupils can be moved between groups easily and teachers can restructure groupings regularly based on their knowledge of pupil progress, levels of achievement, behaviour and rates of work. Different groupings can be adopted for different purposes (Hallam et al., in press).

An alternative to grouping pupils by ability within the class to enable differentiated instruction to take place is to develop a tiered curriculum which enables whole-class exposition but differentiates the work which follows (Ireson, 1998). For instance, one UK school adopted such a system, applying a four-tier system in all subjects in Years 7–13 (Ireson, 1998). The levels were:

- basic – the minimum acceptable for a student of a particular age to achieve
- standard – the average performance expected for a student of a particular age
- extended – above-average performance for a student of a particular age

- advanced – at least one year in advance of an average student of a particular age.

This differentiated structure was used by all departments. All pupils studied the same topic or skill and differentiation was through the level of difficulty. Students selected for themselves the level of work that they wished to attempt, with the teacher negotiating change with the student should the aim prove unrealistic. In the higher age groups pupils were able to select their own set placement. Their choices were invariably realistic. In some lessons, teaching strategies were identical for all tiers; in others they were partly differentiated.

The advantage of the system was that pupils were at the centre of learning within a tightly structured system. There was a common language of achievement used by pupils, parents and teachers, which was clear and simple to understand and provided a framework for planning, reporting and recording. This facilitated cross-subject comparisons and ensured that teachers had accurate perceptions of what pupils could do. Students took responsibility for their own work, acquired considerable meta-cognitive skills, became well motivated, developed a clear understanding of their own capabilities and were encouraged to work independently. Because students selected the levels that they worked at, there was no stigmatisation of the lower ability levels and self-esteem was improved, as was behaviour and overall achievement. The weakness of the system related to the heavy workload for the staff in preparing differentiated materials.

Individualised instruction

While there has been considerable criticism of mixed-ability teaching because of its failure to individualise instruction in the classroom, some systems of individualised instruction have been developed which do operate successfully, particularly with older students. In the USA, the Personalised System of Instruction (PSI), an individualised mastery learning programme, has proved effective for older students in a range of environments. Successful individualised programmes are based on instruction tailored to the assessed abilities of each student; students working at their own pace, receiving periodic reports on their mastery, and planning and evaluating their own learning; and the provision of alternative materials and activities. Where these criteria are satisfied, individualised programmes have been shown to be more effective than whole-class instruction in relation to cognitive and affective outcomes (Waxman *et al.*, 1985).

Learning programmes based on such rigid learning objectives have not proved popular in the UK. However, an individualised programme known as school-based flexible learning has shown considerable promise in geography teaching (Hughes, 1993). Pupils learn through independent study supervised through tutorials, which are regular planned meetings between the teacher and a small group of four to six pupils. The tutorials are used for planning, clarifying, explaining subject specific matters and monitoring general progress and assessment. The key principles underlying the system are that pupils should take increasing responsibility for their learning; teaching and learning take place at an individual level; and that pupils are made aware of how they learn and how specific learning activities contribute (or otherwise) to their progress. For the system to operate effectively, pupils need to receive close support and guidance on a regular, planned basis and teachers need to have access to appropriate resources, including study guides for the topics to be covered.

The system has proved very successful academically and in relation to the personal development of the students. Comparison with parallel classes being taught geography by more traditional methods over a four-year period showed that the percentage of pupils gaining a grade

A to C in geography using flexible learning rose from 41 per cent to 85 per cent. Using traditional methods the increase was from 16 per cent to 59 per cent. The flexible learning system had consistently better results and pupils taught in this way achieved better results in geography than in their other GCSEs. Pupils and their parents reported increased motivation, greater effort and increased work. The students explained this in relation to being given greater responsibility, independence and choice, being able to work at their own pace, not having to go over things they already knew and having access to individual help when they needed it.

For pupils in the later stages of their schooling such individualised teaching methods may be appropriate for some subjects in their entirety and for aspects of others. The ways of working that students develop would not only prepare them for further study at AS, A2 level and beyond but also increase motivation and performance. This seems largely because they have a much greater degree of control over their own learning.

THE LONG-TERM FUTURE

Schools in their present form were designed for the industrial age (Bayliss, 1998). They have been remarkably stable in their structure over the last hundred years and most changes made have been relatively superficial (Cuban, 1990; Sarason, 1990). During that time society has changed. One hundred years ago it was more rigid in its structures – class, gender roles, religious identity – and working practices. Our society is now multi-cultural. Class and religion play a smaller part in the identity formation of most people and gender roles have changed considerably. The nature of work has also changed. Manufacturing industry in the United Kingdom continues to decline, while there has been an increase in the service industries and their availability to customers. As a consequence there are fewer unskilled employment opportunities and a rising demand for a better educated workforce which is literate, numerate and has information-processing skills. Working practices have generally become less rigid, with flexible working hours, more choice of when to take lunch, breaks, holidays, more part-time and hourly paid work and more working from home. These changes in working patterns have not been reflected in school structures and practices. Schools are attempting to provide education for the changing needs of the 21st century in structures designed for the greater rigidity of the 19th. More flexibility is required.

Possible alternatives to rigid structured ability grouping have been outlined in this chapter. In the long term, secondary education will need to become more flexible, offering more diversity in curriculum choice, with greater mixing of vocational and academic options. Schools are likely to be open for longer hours with educational opportunities on offer to whole communities. For this level of flexibility to develop there will need to be changes to the way examinations are currently conceived, with systems becoming less age related and examinations being taken when students have attained the appropriate level. In addition, systems of inspection will need to be more encouraging of innovation to overcome the conservatism that seems inherent in many current school practices.

The evidence suggests that the impetus for changing grouping structures is often external to the school: for instance, Ofsted inspections, government guidance or the appointment of a new head teacher. If schools are to adopt flexible grouping to maximise the academic, personal and social development of their pupils, they need to have ways of monitoring the effectiveness of grouping structures so that change can be instigated internally when necessary. This requires that schools develop ways of systematically monitoring progress across all curriculum subjects, pupils' attitudes towards learning and school, pupils' self-esteem and levels of disaffection (through attendance, unauthorised absence and fixed-term and permanent exclusions). These data can then be used to inform decisions about grouping structures between and within classes. Further information can be gained from the implementation of a properly resourced tutorial system to monitor the progress of individual pupils. If schools adopt such monitoring procedures and act upon the evidence that they provide, there is the very real prospect of grouping structures evolving which are based on the learning needs of pupils rather than administrative convenience. Such learning-focused groupings could play a key role in raising educational attainment.

REFERENCES

Abraham, J. (1989), 'Testing Hargreaves' and Lacey's Differentation-Polarisation Theory in a Setted Comprehensive'. *British Journal of Sociology*, 40 (1), 46–81.

Aitken, M. and Longford, N. (1986), 'Statistical Modelling Issues in School Effectiveness Studies'. *Journal of the Royal Statistical Society*, Series A, 149 (1), 1–43.

Allan, S. (1991), 'Ability Grouping Research Reviews: What do they say about grouping and the gifted?' *Educational Leadership*, 48, 60–65.

Arblaster, G.A., Butler, C., Taylor, A.L, Arnold, C. and Pitchford, M. (1991), 'Same-Age Tutoring, Mastery Learning and the Mixed Ability Teaching of Reading'. *School Psychology International*, 12, 111–118.

Arrowsmith, J. (1989), 'In Search of the Perfect Vintage (Primary and Pre-School)'. *The Times Scottish Educational Supplement*, 1188, 4.

Askew, M. and Wiliam, D. (1995), *Recent Research in Mathematics Education 5–16*. Ofsted reviews of research. London: HMSO.

Ball, S.J. (1981), *Beachside Comprehensive: A case-study of secondary schooling*. Cambridge: Cambridge University Press.

Barker Lunn, J.C. (1970), *Streaming in the Primary School*. Slough: NFER.

— (1984), 'Junior School Teachers: Their methods and practice'. *Educational Research*, 26, 178–188.

Barnes, D., Britton, J. and Rosen, H. (1969), *Language, the Learner and the School*. Harmonsworth: Penguin.

Barnes, D. and Todd, F. (1977), *Communication and Learning in Small Groups*. London: Routledge & Kegan Paul.

Barr, R. and Dreeben, R. (1977), 'Instruction in Classrooms'. In L.S. Shulman (ed.), *Review of Research in Education 5*. Itasca: Peacock.

Bartholomew, H. (2001), *Positioning Students in Setted Mathematics Groups*. Paper presented at the Annual Conference of the British Educational Research Association, University of Leeds, UK, 12–15 September 2001.

Bayliss, V. (1998), *Redefining School*. London: Royal Society for the Encouragement of Arts, Manufactures and Commerce.

Bealing, D. (1972), 'The Organisation of Junior School Classrooms'. *Educational Research,* 14 (3), 231–5.

Benn, C. and Chitty, C. (1996), *Thirty Years On: Is comprehensive education alive and well or struggling to survive?* London: David Fulton Publishers.

Benn, C. and Simon, B. (1970), *Half Way There: Report on the British Comprehensive School Reform.* London: McGraw-Hill.

Bennett, N. (1985), 'Interaction and Achievement in Classroom Groups'. In N. Bennett and C. Desforges (eds.), 'Recent Advances in Classroom Research'. *British Journal of Educational Psychology, Monograph Series,* 2.

— (1991), 'Co-operative Learning in Classrooms: Processes and Outcomes'. *Journal of Child Psychology and Psychiatry,* 32, 581–594.

Bennett, N. and Cass, A. (1989), 'The Effects of Group Composition on Group Interactive Processes and Pupil Understanding'. *British Educational Research Journal,* 15 (1), 19–32.

Bennett, N. and Dunne, E. (1989), *Implementing Co-operative Groupwork in Classrooms.* Exeter: University of Exeter School of Education.

Berends, M. (1995), 'Educational Stratification and Students' Social Bonding to School'. *British Journal of Sociology of Education,* 16 (3), 327–51.

Biggs, J.B. and Moore, P.J. (1993), *The Process of Learning.* Englewood Cliffs: Prentice Hall.

Biott, C. (1987), 'Co-operative Groupwork: Pupils' and teachers' membership and participation'. *Curriculum,* 8 (2) 5–14.

Blandford, J.S (1958), 'Standardised Tests in Junior Schools with Special Reference to the Effects of Streaming on the Constancy of Results'. *British Journal of Educational Psychology,* 28, 170–3.

Block, N. and Dworkin, G. (eds.) (1976), *The IQ Controversy.* New York: Pantheon.

Bloom, B.S. (1976), *Human Characteristics and School Learning.* New York: McGraw-Hill.

— (1984a), 'The 2 Sigma Problem: The search for methods of instruction as effective as one-to-one tutoring'. *Educational Researcher,* 13 (6), 4–16.

— (1984b), 'The Search for Methods of Group Instruction as Effective as One-to-One Tutoring'. *Educational Leadership,* 41 (8), 4–17.

Boaler, J. (1997a), 'Setting, Social Class and the Survival of the Quickest'. *British Educational Research Journal,* 23, 575–595.

— (1997b), 'When Even the Winners are Losers: Evaluating the experiences of "top set" students'. *Journal of Curriculum Studies*, 29, 165–182.

— (1997c), *Experiencing School Mathematics: Teaching styles, sex and setting.* Buckingham: Open University Press.

Boaler, J., Wiliam, D. and Brown, M. (2000), 'Experiences of Ability Grouping –Disaffection, polarisation and the construction of failure'. *British Educational Research Journal*, 28 (5), 631–648.

Board of Education (Great Britain) (1931), *The Primary School.* London: HMSO.

Bossert, S.T. (1988), 'Co-operative Activities in the Classroom'. *Review of Research in Education*, 15, 225–250.

Bouri, J. and Barker Lunn, J. (1969), *Too Small to Stream: A study of grouping in small junior schools.* Slough: NFER.

Brody, N. (1985), 'The Validity of Intelligence'. In B.B. Wolman (ed.), *Handbook of Intelligence.* New York: John Wiley and Son.

Burden, M., Emsley, M. and Constable, M. (1988), 'Encouraging Progress in Collaborative Groupwork'. *Education 3–13*, 16 (1), 51–6.

Burgess, R.G. (1983), *Experiencing Comprehensive Education: A study of Bishop McGregor School.* London: Methuen.

— (1984), 'It's Not a Proper Subject: It's just Newsom'. In I. Goodson and S. Ball (eds.), *Defining the Curriculum.* London: Falmer.

— (1986), *Education, Schools and Society.* London: Batsford.

Burns, R. (1987), 'Steering Groups, Levelling Effects, and Instructional Pace'. *American Journal of Education*, 96 (1), 24–56.

Byrne, B.M. (1988), 'Adolescent Self-Concept, Ability Grouping and Social Comparison: Re-examining academic track differences in high school'. *Youth and Society*, 20, 46–67.

Carroll, J.B. (1963), 'A Model of School Learning'. *Teacher College Record*, 64, 723–733.

Ceci, S.J. (1990), *On Intelligence …More or Less: A biological treatise on intellectual development.* Englewood Cliffs: Prentice Hall.

Chaplain, R. (1996), 'Pupils Under Pressure: Coping with stress at school'. In J. Rudduck, R. Chaplain and G. Wallace (eds.), *School Improvement: What can pupils tell us?* London: David Fulton Publishers.

Chapman, J.W. (1988), 'Learning Disabled Children's Self-Concepts'. *Review of Educational Research*, 58, 347–371.

Chauvet, M. and Blatchford, P. (1993), 'Group Composition and National Curriculum Assessment at Seven Years'. *Educational Research*, 35 (2), 189–196.

Chubb, J. and Moe, T. (1990), *Politics, Markets and America's Schools*. Washington DC: The Brookings Institution.

Cicourel, A. and Kitsuse, J. (1963), *The Educational Decision-Makers*. Indianapolis: The Bobbs Merrill Company.

Clammer, R. (1985), 'Mixed Ability Teaching: Meanings and motives. A study of two geography departments'. *SERCH*, 7, 17–19.

Codling, D. (1975), *Slow Learners in the Secondary School*. Birmingham: Birmingham Association of the National Union of Teachers.

Cohen, E.G. (1994), 'Restructuring the Classroom: Conditions for productive small groups'. *Review of Educational Research*, 64, 1–35.

Commission for Racial Equality (1992), *Set to Fail? Setting and banding in secondary schools*. London: Commission for Racial Equality.

Creemers, B.P.M. (1994), *The Effective Classroom*. London: Cassell.

Crozier, S. and Kleinberg, S. (1987), 'Solving Problems in a Group'. *Education 3–13*, 15 (3), 37–41.

Cuban, L. (1990), 'A Fundamental Puzzle of School Reform'. In A. Leiberman (ed.), *Schools as Collaborative Structures: Creating the future now*. New York: Falmer Press.

Cuttance, P. (1992), 'Evaluating the Effectiveness of Schools'. In D. Reynolds and P. Cuttance (eds.), *School Effectiveness: Research, policy and practice*. London: Cassell.

Daniels, J.C. (1961a), 'The Effects of Streaming in the Primary Schools: 1. What teachers believe'. *British Journal of Educational Psychology*, 31, 69–78.

— (1961b), 'The Effects of Streaming in the Primary Schools: 2. Comparison of streamed and unstreamed schools'. *British Journal of Educational Psychology*, 31, 119–26.

Dar, Y. (1985), 'Teachers' Attitudes Toward Ability Grouping: Educational considerations and social and organisational influences'. *Interchange*, 16 (2), 17–38.

Davies, R.P. (1975), *Mixed Ability Grouping*. London: Temple Smith.

Deitrich, F.R. (1964), 'Comparison of Sixth Grade Pupils in Two School Systems: Ability grouping compared to heterogeneous grouping'. *Journal of Educational Research*, 57, 507–512.

Dentzer, E. and Wheelock, A. (1990), *Locked In/Locked Out: Tracking and placement in Boston public schools*. Boston: The Massachusetts Advocacy Center.

Department for Education (1993), 'Improving Primary Education – Patten'. *DfE News*, 16/93. London: DfE.

Department for Education and Employment (1997), *Excellence in Schools*. Cm 3681. London: HMSO.

— (1998), *The National Literacy Strategy*. London: HMSO.

Department for Education and Employment and Qualifications and Curriculum Authority (1999), *The National Curriculum*. London: DfEE/QCA.

Department for Education and Science (1978), *Primary Education in England: A survey by HM Inspectors of Schools*. London: HMSO.

— (1989), *Behaviour in Schools* (The Elton Report). London: HMSO.

— (1991), *National Curriculum and Special Needs: Preparations to implement the National Curriculum for pupils with statements in special and ordinary schools, 1989–90: A report by HM Inspectorate*. London: DfES.

— (1992), *The Education of Very Able Children in Maintained Schools: A review by HMI*. London: HMSO.

Devine, D. (1993), 'A Study of Reading Ability Groups: Primary school children's experiences and views'. *Irish Educational Studies*, 12, 134–42.

Douglas, J.F. (1973), 'A Study of Streaming at a Grammar School'. *Educational Research*, 15, 140–143.

Douglas, J.W.B. (1964), *The Home and the School*. London: MacGibbon and Kee.

Douglas, J.W.B., Ross, J.M. and Simpson, H.R. (1968), *All Our Futures*. London: Peter Davies.

Draisey, A.G. (1985), 'Vertical Grouping in the Primary School – A positive view'. *Education Development*, 9 (1), 3–11.

Dreeben, R. and Barr, R. (1988), 'Classroom Composition and the Design of Instruction'. *Sociology of Education*, 61, 129–142.

Dunne, E. and Bennett, N. (1990), *Talking and Learning in Groups*. London: Macmillan.

Eilam, B. and Finegold, M. (1992), 'The Heterogeneous Class: A solution: Or just another problem?' *Studies in Educational Evaluation*, 18 (2), 265–78.

Entwistle, N.J. (1981), *Styles of Learning and Teaching*. New York: John Wiley and Sons.

Esposito, D. (1973), 'Homogenous and Heterogenous Ability Grouping: Principal findings and implications for evaluating and designing more effective educational environments'. *Review of Educational Research*, 43 (2), 163–79.

Essen, J., Fogelman, K. and Tibbenham, A. (1978), 'Some Non-Academic Developmental Correlates of Ability-Grouping in Secondary Schools'. *Educational Studies*, 5 (1), 83–93.

Evertson, C.M. (1982), 'Differences in Instructional Activities in Higher and Lower Achieving Junior High English and Math Classes'. *Elementary School Journal*, 82, 219–232.

Feldusen, J.F. (1989), 'Synthesis of Research on Gifted Youth'. *Educational Leadership*, 46 (6), 6–11.

Ferri, E. (1971), *Streaming Two Years Later: A follow up of a group of pupils who attended streamed and nonstreamed junior schools*. London: NFER.

Feuerstein, R., Rand, Y., Hoffman, M.B. and Miller, R. (1980), *Instrumental Enrichment: An intervention program for cognitive modifiability*. Baltimore: University Park.

Findlay, W. and Bryan, M. (1975), 'The Pros and Cons of Ability Grouping'. *Phi Delta Kappan*, 66, 12.

Finley, M.K. (1984), 'Teachers and Tracking in a Comprehensive High School'. *Sociology of Education*, 57, 233–243.

Fogelman, K. (1983), 'Ability Grouping in the Secondary School'. In K. Fogelman (ed.), *Growing Up in Great Britain: Papers from the National Child Development Study*. London: Macmillan for the National Children's Bureau.

Fogelman, K., Essen, J. and Tibbenham, A. (1978), 'Ability Grouping in Secondary Schools and Attainment'. *Educational Studies*, 4 (3), 201–212.

Fogelman, K. and Goldstein, H. (1976), 'Social Factors Associated with Changes in Educational Attainment Between 7 and 11 Years of Age'. *Educational Studies*, 2, 95–109.

Ford, J. (1969), *Social Class and the Comprehensive School*. London: Routledge & Kegan Paul.

Frost, A.W. (1978), 'Mixed Ability Versus Streaming in Science – A controlled experiment'. *School Science Review*, 60, 347–350.

Galloway, D. (1983), 'Disruptive Pupils and Effective Pastoral Care'. *School Organisation*, 13, 245–54.

Galton, M. (1981), 'Teaching Groups in the Junior School: A neglected art'. *Schools Organisation*, 1 (2), 175–81.

— (1987), 'An ORACLE Chronicle: A decade of classroom research'. *Teaching and Teacher Education*, 3 (4), 299–314.

— (1989), *Primary Teaching*. London: David Fulton.

— (1990), 'Grouping and Group Work'. In C. Rogers and P. Kutnick, *The Social Psychology of the Primary School*. London: Routledge.

Galton, M., Patrick, H., Appleyard, R., Hargreaves, L. and Bernbaum, G. (1987), *Curriculum Provision in Small Schools: The PRISMS project, final report*. Leicester: University of Leicester.

Galton, M., Simon, B. and Croll, P. (1980), *Inside the Primary Classroom*. London: Routledge & Kegan Paul.

Galton, M. and Williamson, J. (1992), *Groupwork in the Primary Classroom*. London: Routledge.

Gamoran, A. (1986), 'Instructional and Institutional Effects of Ability Grouping'. *Sociology of Education*, 59, 185–198.

— (1989), 'Measuring Curriculum Differentiation'. *American Journal of Education*, 97, 129–143.

— (1990), *The Consequences of Track-Related Instructional Differences for Student Achievement*. Paper presented at the Annual Meeting of the American Educational Research Association, Boston, USA, 1990.

Gamoran, A. and Berends, M. (1987), 'The Effects of Stratification in Secondary Schools: Synthesis of survey and ethnographic research'. *Review of Educational Research*, 57, 415–435.

Gamoran, A. and Mare, R.D. (1989), 'Secondary School Tracking and Educational Inequality: Compensation, reinforcement or neutrality?' *American Journal of Sociology*, 94, 1146–1183.

Gardner, H. (1993), *Frames of Mind: The theory of multiple intelligences*. New York: Basic Books.

— (1999), 'Are There Additional Intelligences? The case for naturalist, spiritual and existential intelligences'. In J. Kane (ed.), *Education, Information and Transformation*. Englewood Cliffs: Prentice Hall.

George, P. (1989), *The Japanese Junior High School: A view from the inside*. Columbus: National Middle School Association.

Gillborn, D. and Youdell, D. (2000), *Rationing Education: Policy, practice, reform and equity*. Buckingham: Open University Press.

Glaye, A. (1986), 'Outer Appearances With Inner Experiences – Towards a more holistic view of group-work'. *Educational Review*, 38 (1), 45–56.

Goleman, D. (1996), *Emotional Intelligence: Why it can matter more than IQ*. London: Bloomsbury.

Goodlad, J.I. (ed.) (1989), *Access to Knowledge*. New York: College Entrance Examination Board.

Gray, J., McPherson, A. and Raffe, D. (1983), *Reconstructions of Secondary Education*. London: Routledge & Kegan Paul.

Gray, J., Jesson, D. and Jones, B. (1986), 'The Search for a Fairer Way of Comparing Schools' Examination Results'. *Research Papers in Education*, 10 (1), 91–122.

Gregory, R.P. (1984), 'Streaming, Setting and Mixed Ability Grouping in Primary and Secondary Schools: Some research findings'. *Educational Studies*, 10 (3), 209–226.

— (1986), 'Mixed Ability Teaching – A rod for the teacher's back?' *Journal of Applied Educational Studies*, 15 (2), 56–61.

Gregory, R.P., Hackney, C. and Gregory, N.M. (1982), 'Corrective Reading Programme: An evaluation'. *British Journal of Educational Psychology*, 52, 33–50.

Gregson, A. and Quinn, W.F. (1978), 'Mixed Ability Methods and Educational Standards'. *Comprehensive Education*, 37, 12–16.

Guskey, T.R. and Gates, S.L. (1985), *A Synthesis of Research on Group-Based Mastery Learning Programs*. Paper presented at the Annual Meeting of the American Educational Research Association, Chicago, USA, 1985.

Gutierrez, R. and Slavin, R.E. (1992), 'Achievement Effects of the Non-Graded Elementary School: A best evidence synthesis'. *Review of Educational Research*, 62, 333–376.

Guttman, Y., Gur, A., Daniel, S. and Well, D. (1972), The Effects of Ability Grouping on *Learning Achievements and Psychosocial Development*. Jerusalem: Szold Institute.

Hacker, R.G. and Rowe, M.J. (1985), 'A Study of Teaching and Learning Processes in Integrated Science Classrooms'. *International Journal of Science Education*, 7, 173–180.

— (1993), 'A Study of the Effects of an Organisation Change from Streamed to Mixed-Ability Classes Upon Science Classroom Instruction'. *Journal of Research in Science Teaching*, 30 (3), 223–231.

Hacker, R.G., Rowe, M.J. and Evans, R.D. (1991), 'The Influences of Ability Groupings for Secondary Science Lessons Upon Classroom Processes. Part 1: Homogeneous groupings (Science Education Notes)'. *School Science Review*, 73 (262), 125–9.

Hadow Report/Great Britain Board of Education Consultative Committee on the Primary School (1930), *The Primary School*. London: HMSO.

Hallam, S. (1996), *Improving School Attendance*. Oxford: Heinemann.

— (1998), *Instrumental Teaching: A practical guide to better teaching and learning*. Oxford: Heinemann.

Hallam, S. and Castle, F. (1999), *Evaluation of the Behaviour and Discipline Pilot Projects (1996–99) Supported under the Standards Fund Programme*. London: DfEE.

Hallam, S. and Deathe, K. (in press), 'Ability Grouping and Changes in Self-Concept through Key Stages 3 and 4'. Westminster Studies in Education.

Hallam, S. and Ireson, J. (1999), 'Pedagogy in the Secondary School'. In P. Mortimore (ed.), *Understanding Pedagogy and its Impact on Learning*. London: Sage Publications.

— (in press), 'Secondary School Teachers' Attitudes to and Beliefs About Ability Grouping'. *British Journal of Educational Psychology*.

— (unpublished, a), 'The Effects of Different Kinds of Ability Grouping on Pedagogy in the Secondary School'.

— (unpublished, b), 'Subject Domain Differences in Teachers' Beliefs About Ability Grouping and their Effects on Pedagogy'.

Hallam, S., Ireson, J., Chaudhury, I., Lister, V., Davies, J. and Mortimore, P. (1999), *Ability Grouping Practices in the Primary School: A survey of what schools are doing*. Paper presented at the British Research Association Conference, University of Sussex, UK, 2–5 September 1999.

Hallam, S., Ireson, J. and Davies, J. (unpublished), 'Primary School Pupils' Experience of Different Types of Grouping in School'.

Hallam, S., Ireson, J. and Davies, J. (in press), *Effective Pupil Grouping in the Primary School: A practical guide*. London: David Fulton Publishers.

Hallam, S., Ireson, J., Davies, J. and Mortimore, P. (1999a), *Ability Grouping Practices in the Primary School: Pedagogic practices*. Paper presented at the British Psychological Society Education Section Conference, University of Greenwich, UK, 6–7 November 1999.

— (1999b), *School Ethos and Primary Pupils' Perceptions of Ability Grouping*. Paper presented at the British Research Association Conference, University of Sussex, UK, 2–5 September 1999.

Hallam, S., Ireson, J. and Hurley, C. (unpublished, a), 'Experiences of Ability Grouping in the Secondary School 1: Pupils' voices'.

— (unpublished, b), 'Experiences of Ability Grouping in the Secondary School 2: Pupil preferences and rationales'.

— (2001a), *Ability Grouping in the Secondary School: Pupils' experiences of different grouping practices*. Paper presented at the British Educational Research Association Conference, University of Leeds, UK, 12–15 September 2001.

— (2001b), *Subject Domain Differences in Teachers' Beliefs about Ability Grouping and their Effects on Pedagogy*. Paper presented at the Annual Conference of the British Educational Research Association, University of Leeds, UK, 12–15 September 2001.

Hallam, S., Ireson, J., Lister, V., Andon Chaudhury, I. and Davies, J. (unpublished), 'Grouping Practices in the Primary School: What influences change?'

Hallam, S., Ireson, J. and Mortimore, P. (2000), *Children's Socialisation into Schools' Learning Contexts: Ability grouping in the UK primary school*. Roundtable paper presented at the annual conference of AERA, New Orleans, USA, 24–28 April 2000.

Hallam, S., Ireson, J., Mortimore, P., Hack, S. and Clark, H. (1999), *Teachers' Views of Ability Grouping in English Secondary Schools*. Paper presented at the 8th European Conference for Research on Learning and Instruction, Goteborg University, Sweden, 24–28 August 1999.

Hallam, S. and Toutounji, I. (1996a), *What Do We Know About the Grouping of Pupils by Ability?* London: Institute of Education, University of London.

— (1996b), 'What Do We Know About Grouping Pupils by Ability?' *Education Review*, 10 (2), 62–70.

Hallinan, M. and Sorensen, A. (1985), 'Ability Grouping and Student Friendships'. *American Educational Research Journal*, 22, 485–499.

Hallinan, M. and Williams, R. (1989), 'Interracial Friendship Choices in Secondary Schools'. *American Sociological Review*, 54, 67–78.

Hargreaves, D.H. (1967), *Social Relations in a Secondary School*. London: Tinling.

Harlen, W. and Malcolm, H. (1997), *Setting and Streaming: A research review*. Using Research Series, 18. Edinburgh: SCRE.

Harris, A. (2000), 'Effective Leadership and Departmental Improvement'. *Westminster Studies in Education*, 23, 81–90.

— (2001), 'Department Improvement and School Improvement: A missing link?' *British Educational Research Journal*, 27 (4), 477–486.

Hart, R.H. (1962), 'The Nongraded Primary School and Arithmetic'. *The Arithmetic Teacher*, 9, 130–133.

Harvey, T.J. (1981), 'The Correlation Between IQ, Science Achievement and Gender of Secondary School Students When Taught in Mixed Ability Groups'. *The Australian Science Teachers Association*, 27 (2), 89–94.

Harwood, D. (1989), 'The Nature of Teacher-Pupil Interaction in the Active Tutorial Work Approach: Using interaction analysis to evaluate student-centred approaches'. *British Educational Research Journal*, 15, 177–194.

— (1995), 'The Pedagogy of the World Studies 8–13 Project: The influence of the presence/absence of the teacher upon primary children's collaborative work'. *British Educational Research Journal*, 21 (5), 587–612.

Hauge, T.E. (1974), *Skolemiljo og Elevholdninger*. Trondheim: TAPIR.

HMI Department of Education and Science (1978), *Mixed Ability Work in Comprehensive Schools*. London: HMSO.

— (1979), *Aspects of Secondary Education in England*. London: HMSO.

— (1992), *The Education of Very Able Children in Maintained Schools*. London: HMSO.

Hughes, M. (1993), *Flexible Learning: Evidence examined*. Stafford: Network Educational Press Ltd.

Husen, T. and Boalt, G. (1967), *Educational Research and Educational Change: The case of Sweden*. Stockholm: Almquist.

Ingleson, S. (1982), 'Creating Conditions for Success With Mixed Ability Classes'. In M.K. Sands and T. Kerry (eds.), *Mixed Ability Teaching*. London: Croom Helm.

Ingram, V. (1960), 'Fling Evaluates its Primary Cycle'. *Elementary School Journal*, 61, 76–80.

Ireson, J. (1998), *Innovative Grouping Practices in Secondary Schools*. London: DfEE.

Ireson, J. and Hallam, S. (1999), 'Raising Standards: Is ability grouping the answer?' *Oxford Review of Education*, 25 (3), 343–358.

— (2000/1), 'Getting to Grips With Grouping: Principles and practicalities'. *Curriculum Management Update*, 11, 4.

— (2001), *Ability Grouping in Education*. London: Sage Publications.

Ireson, J., Hallam, S., Hack, S., Clark, H. and Plewis, I. (in press), 'Ability Grouping in English, Mathematics and Science: Effects on pupil attainment'. *Journal of Educational Research and Evaluation*.

Ireson, J., Hallam, S. and Hurley, C. (2001), *Pupils' Relationships with School: Does ability grouping make a difference?* Paper presented at the BPS Developmental and Education Sections' joint conference, University College Worcester, UK, 6–9 September 2001.

Ireson, J., Hallam, S., Mortimore, P., Hack, S., Clark, H. and Plewis, I (1999), *Ability Grouping in English, Mathematics and Science: Effects on pupil attainment*. Paper presented at the BPS Education Section Conference, University of Greenwich, UK, 6–7 November 1999.

Ireson, J., Hallam, S. and Plewis, I. (2001), 'Ability Grouping in Secondary Schools: Effects on pupils' self-concepts'. *British Journal of Educational Psychology*, 71, 315–326.

Jackson, B. (1964), *Streaming: An education system in miniature*. London: Routledge & Kegan Paul.

Jenson, A.R. (1970), 'Another Look at Culture-Fair Testing'. In J. Helmuth (ed.), *The Disadvantaged Child*. New York: Brunner-Mazel.

Jesson, D. (2000), *Further Evidence on Comparative GCSE Performance Between Selective and Non-Selective Schools and LEAs*. Paper presented at the NUT Secondary Education Conference, March 2000.

Johannesson, I. (1962), 'School Differentiation and Social Adjustment of Pupils'. *Educational Research*, 4, 133–139.

Johnson, D.W. and Johnson, R.T. (1990), 'Co-operative learning and achievement'. In S. Sharan (ed.), *Co-operative Learning: Theory and research*. New York: Praeger.

Keddie, N. (1971), 'Classroom Knowledge'. In M.F.D. Young (ed.), *Knowledge and Control*. London: Collier-Macmillan.

Keller, F.S. (1968), 'Goodbye Teacher ...'. *Journal of Applied Behavioural Analysis*, 1, 79–89.

Kerckhoff, A. (1986), 'Effects of Ability Grouping in British Secondary Schools'. *American Sociological Review*, 51, 842–858.

Kerckhoff, A.C., Fogelman, K., Crook, D. and Reeder, D. (1996), *Going Comprehensive in England and Wales: A study of uneven change*. London: Woburn Press.

Kerry, T. (1980a), 'Provision for Bright Pupils in 40 Schools: Three years' progress'. *Cambridge Journal of Education*, 10 (3), 134–43.

— (1980b), 'RE: A Suitable Case for Mixed Ability?' *British Journal of Religious Education*, 3 (2), 46–52.

— (1982a), 'Providing for Slow Learners'. *Special Education: Forward trends*, 8 (4), 9–11.

— (1982b), 'The Demands Made by RE on Pupils' Thinking'. In J. Hull (ed.), *New Directions in Religious Education*. Lewes, Sussex: Falmer Press.

— (1982c), *Teachers' Identification of Exceptional Pupils and their Strategies for Coping With Them*. PhD thesis, University of Nottingham.

— (1984), 'Analysing the Cognitive Demand Made by Classroom Tasks in Mixed-Ability Classes'. In E.C. Wragg, *Classroom Teaching Skills: The research findings of the teacher education project*. London: Routledge.

Kerry, T. and Sands, M.K. (1984), 'Classroom Organisation and Learning'. In E.C. Wragg, *Classroom Teaching Skills: The research findings of the teacher education project*. London: Routledge.

Kulik, C-L.C. and Kulik, J.A. (1982a), 'Effects of Ability Grouping on Secondary School Students: A meta-analysis of evaluation findings'. *American Educational Research Journal*, 19, 415–428.

— (1982b), 'Research Synthesis on Ability Grouping'. *Educational Leadership*, 39, 619–621.

— (1990), 'Effectiveness of Mastery Learning Programmes: A meta-analysis'. *Review of Educational Research*, 60, 265–299.

Kulik, J.A. (1991), *Ability Grouping*. Research-based decision making series. Storrs: National Research Center on the Gifted and Talented, University of Connecticut.

Kulik, J.A. and Kulik, C-L.C. (1984), 'Effects of Accelerated Instruction on Students'. *Reviews of Educational Research*, 54, 409–426.

— (1986), *Operative and Interpretable Effect Sizes in Meta-Analysis*. Paper presented at the Annual Meeting of the American Educational Research Association, San Francisco, 1986.

— (1987), 'Effects of Ability Grouping on Student Achievement'. *Equity and Excellence*, 23 (1–2), 22–30.

— (1991), 'Ability Grouping and Gifted Students'. In N. Colangelo and G. Davis (eds.), *Handbook of Gifted Education*. Boston: Allyn & Bacon.

— (1992), 'Meta-Analytic Findings on Grouping Programs'. *Gifted Child Quarterly*, 36 (2), 73–77.

van Laarhoven, P. and de Vries, A. (1987), 'Effects of Heterogeneous Grouping in Secondary Schools'. In J. Scheerends and W. Stoel (eds.), *Effectiveness of School Organisations*. Lisse: Swets & Zeitlinger.

Lacey, C. (1970), *Hightown Grammar*. Manchester: Manchester University Press.

— (1974), 'Destreaming in a "Pressured" Academic Environment'. In J. Eggleston (ed.), *Contemporary Research in the Sociology of Education*. London: Methuen.

Lai, P. and Biggs, J. (1994), 'Who Benefits from Mastery Learning?' *Contemporary Educational Psychology*, 19, 12–23.

Lawrence, F. and Munch, T.W. (1984), 'The Effects of Grouping of Laboratory Students on Selected Educational Outcomes'. *Journal of Research in Science Teaching*, 21, 699–708.

Lee, J. and Croll, P. (1995), 'Streaming and Subject Specialism at Key Stage 2: A survey in two local authorities'. *Educational Studies*, 21 (2), 155–65.

Levine, D.U. (1992), 'An Interpretative Review of US Research and Practice Dealing With Unusually Effective Schools'. In D. Reynolds and P. Cuttance (eds.), *School Effectiveness: Research, policy and practice*. London: Cassell.

Levine D.U. and Lezotte, L.W. (1990), *Unusually Effective Schools: A review and analysis of research and practice*. Madison: National Center for Effective Schools Research and Development.

Lou, Y., Abrami, P.C., Spence, J.C., Poulsen, C., Chambers, B. and d'Apollonia, S. (1996), 'Within-Class Grouping: A meta-analysis'. *Review of Educational Research*, 66 (4), 423–58.

Lughart, E., Roeders, P.J.B., Bosker, R.J. and Bos, K.T. (1989), *Effectieve School-Kenmerken in het Voortgezet Onderwijs'. Deel 1: Literatuurstudie (Effective schools' characteristics in secondary education. Part 1: Literature review)*. Gronigen: RION.

Lysakowski, R. and Walberg, H. (1982), 'Instructional Effects of Cues, Participation, and Corrective Feedback: A quantitative synthesis'. *American Educational Research Journal*, 19, 559–578.

Mac an Ghaill, M. (1988), *Young, Gifted and Black: Student-teacher relations in the schooling of black youth*. Milton Keynes: Open University Press.

Maguire, M., Maguire, S. and Felstead, A. (1993), *Factors Influencing Individual Commitment to Lifetime Learning: A literature review*. Leicester: Centre for Labour Market Studies.

Marascuilo, L.A. and McSweeney, M. (1972), 'Tracking and Minority Student Attitudes and Performance'. *Urban Education*, 6, 303–319.

Marks, J. (1991), *Standards in Schools*. London: Social Market Foundation.

Marks, J., Cox, C. and Pomian-Srzednicki, M. (1983), *Standards in English Schools: An analysis of examination results of secondary schools in England for 1981*. London: National Council for Educational Standards.

Marsh, H.W. (1991), 'The Failure of High-Ability High Schools to Deliver Academic Benefits: The importance of academic self-concept and educational aspirations'. *American Educational Research Journal*, 28, 445–480.

Marsh, H.W., Chessor, D., Craven, R.G. and Roche, L. (1995), 'The Effects of Gifted and Talented Programs on Academic Self-Concept: The big fish strikes again'. *American Educational Research Journal*, 32, 285–319.

Marsh, H.W., Parker, J. and Barnes, J. (1985), 'Multidimensional Adolescent Self-Concepts: Their relationship to age, sex and academic measures'. *American Educational Research Journal*, 22, 422–444.

Marsh, H.W. and Peart, N. (1988), 'Competitive and Co-operative Physical Fitness Training Programs for Girls: Effects on physical fitness and on multidimensional self-concepts'. *Journal of Sport and Exercise Psychology*, 10, 390–407.

Marsh, H.W. and Rowe, K.J. (1996), 'The Negative Effects of School-Average Ability on Academic Self-Concept: An application of multilevel modelling'. *Australian Journal of Education*, 40 (1), 65–87.

Marsh, H.W. and Yeung, A.S. (1997), 'Course Work Selection: Relations to academic self-concept and achievement'. *American Educational Research Journal*, 34 (4), 691–720.

Maughan, B. and Rutter, M. (1987), 'Pupils' Progress in Selective and Non-Selective Schools'. *School Organization*, 7 (1), 49–68.

McDermott, J.W. (1976), *The Controversy Over Ability Grouping in American Education, 1916–1970*. Doctoral dissertation, Temple University, Philadelphia.

McGivney, V. (1992), *Tracking Adult Learning Routes*. Leicester: NIACE.

McGuiness, C. (1999), *From Thinking Skills to Thinking Classrooms*. London: DfEE.

McPherson, A. and Willms, D. (1987), *Equalisation and Improvement: Some effects of comprehensive organisation in Scotland*. Paper presented to the Annual Meeting of the American Educational Research Association, May 1987.

Metz, M.H. (1978), *Classrooms and Corridors: The crisis of authority in desegregated secondary schools*. Berkeley: University of California Press.

Metz, M. (1983), 'Sources of Constructive Social Relationships in an Urban Magnet Middle School'. *American Journal of Education*, 91, 202–245.

Miller, B.A. (1990), 'A Review of the Quantitative Research on Multi-Grade Instruction'. *Research in Rural Education*, 7 (1), 1–8.

Ministry of Education (Israel) (1965), *Survey of Grouping*. Jerusalem: The Pedagogic Secretariat (Hebrew).

Mirza, H.S. (1992), *Young, Female and Black*. London: Routledge.

Mortimore, P., Sammons, P., Ecob, R., Stoll, L. and Lewis, D. (1988), *School Matters: The junior years*. Salisbury: Open Books.

Mortimore, P., Sammons, P., Stoll, L., Lewis, D. and Ecob, R. (1988), *The Junior School Project*. London: ILEA Research & Statistics.

Murphy, P. and Elwood, J. (1998), 'Gendered Experiences, Choices and Achievement – Exploring the links'. *International Journal of Inclusive Education*, 2 (2), 95–118.

National Education Association (1968), *Ability Grouping: Research summary.* Washington: NEA.

Neave, G. (1975), *How They Fared: The impact of the comprehensive school on the university.* London: Routledge & Kegan Paul.

Newbold, D. (1977), *Ability Grouping: The Banbury Enquiry.* Slough: National Foundation for Educational Research Publishing Company Ltd.

Nuttall, D., Goldstein, H., Prosser, R. and Rasbash, J. (1989), 'Differential School Effectiveness'. *International Journal of Educational Research,* 13 (7), 769–76.

Oakes, J. (1982), 'The Reproduction of Inequity: The content of secondary school tracking'. *The Urban Review,* 14 (2), 107–120.

— (1985), *Keeping Track: How schools structure inequality.* New Haven: Yale University Press.

— (1990), *Multiplying Inequalities: The effects of race, social class, and tracking on opportunities to learn mathematics and science.* Santa Monica: RAND.

— (1992), 'Can Tracking Research Inform Practice? Technical, normative and political considerations'. *Educational Researcher,* 12–21.

Oakes, J., Gamoran, A. and Page, R. (1991), 'Curriculum Differentiation: Opportunities, consequences and meanings'. In P. Jackson (ed.), *Handbook of Research on Curriculum.* New York: Macmillan.

Oakes, J., Slevin, M., Karoly, L. and Guiton, G. (1992), *Educational Match Making: Academic and vocational tracking in comprehensive high schools.* Santa Monica: RAND.

Office for Standards in Education (1993), *Access and Achievement in Urban Education.* London: Ofsted.

— (1994), *Primary Matters: A discussion on teaching and learning in primary schools.* London: Ofsted.

— (1995), *Annual Report of Her Majesty's Chief Inspector of Schools, 1993/4: Part 1, Standards and quality in education.* London: OFSTED.

— (1997), *The Annual Report of her Majesty's Chief Inspector of Schools: Standards and quality in education 1995/6.* London: The Stationery Office.

— (1998a), *The Annual Report of her Majesty's Chief Inspector of Schools: Standards and quality in education 1996/7.* London: The Stationery Office.

— (1998b), *Setting in Primary Schools: A report from the Office of her Majesty's Chief Inspector of Schools.* London: Ofsted.

Opdenakker, M.C. and Van Damme, J. (2001), 'Relationship Between School Composition and Characteristics of School Process and their Effect on Mathematics Achievement'. *British Educational Research Journal*, 27 (4), 407–432.

Oygarden, S., Lunde, O. and Jorgensen, H. (1971), *Grisgrendtprosjektet: Trivsel og tilpasning i ulike ungdomsskolemiljo*. Preliminary report.

Page, R.N. (1984), *Perspectives and Processes: The negotiation of educational meaning in high school classes for academically unsuccessful students*. Unpublished PhD dissertation, University of Wisconsin.

Page, R. (1992), *Lower Track Classrooms: A curricular and cultural perspective*. New York: Teachers College Press.

Pallas, A.M., Entwisle, D.R., Alexander, K.L. and Stluka, M.F. (1994), 'Ability-Group Effects: Instructional, social, or institutional?' *Sociology of Education*, 67 (1), 27–46.

Parkinson, B.L., Mitchell, R.F. and Johnstone, R.M. (1983), 'Mastery Learning in Modern Languages – A case study'. *PLET*, 20 (1), 43–53.

Passow, A. (1988), 'Issues of Access to Knowledge: Grouping and tracking'. In L. Tanner (ed.), *Critical Issues in Curriculum*. Chicago: University of Chicago Press.

Peak, B. and Morrison, K. (1988), 'Investigating Banding Origins and Destinations in a Comprehensive School'. *School Organisation*, 8 (3), 339–349.

Peverett, R. (1994), 'Teaching 9–11 Year Olds'. In National Commission of Education, *Insights into Education and Training*. Oxford: Heinemann.

Plewes, J.A. (1979), 'Mixed Ability Teaching: A deterioration in performance'. *Journal of Research in Science Teaching*, 16, 229–236.

Plomin, R. (1986), *Development, Genetics and Psychology*. Hillsdale: LEA.

Plomin, R. and Thompson, L.E. (1993), 'Genetics and High Cognitive Ability'. In G.R. Bock and K. Ackrill (eds.), *The Origins and Development of High Ability*. New York: John Wiley and Sons.

Plowden Report – DES/CACE (1967), *Children and their Primary Schools*. London: HMSO.

Postlethwaite, K. and Denton, C. (1978), *Streams for the Future: The long-term effects of early streaming and non-streaming – the final report of the Banbury Enquiry*. Banbury: Pubansco Publications.

Pratt, D. (1986), 'On the Merits of Multi-Age Classrooms'. *Research in Rural Education*, 3 (3), 111–115.

Raudenbush, S.W., Rowan, B., and Cheong, Y.F. (1992), 'Contextual Effects on the Self-Perceived Efficacy of High School Teachers'. *Sociology of Education*, 65, 150–167.

Reid, K., Hopkins, D. and Holly, P. (1987), *Towards the Effective School*. Oxford: Blackwell.

Reid, M.E., Clunies-Ross, L.R., Goacher, B. and Vile, D. (1982), *Mixed Ability Teaching: Problems and possibilities*. Windsor: NFER-Nelson.

Reuman, D.A. (1989), 'How Social Comparison Mediates the Relation Between Ability-Grouping Practices and Students' Achievement Expectancies in Mathematics'. *Journal of Educational Psychology*, 81, 178–189.

Reynolds, D. (1982), 'The Search for Effective Schools'. *School Organisation*, 2 (3), 215–237.

Reynolds, D., Sullivan, M. and Murgatroyd, S. (1987), *The Comprehensive Experiment: A comparison of the selective and non-selective system of school organization*. London: Falmer Press.

Rist, R. (1970), 'Student Social Class and Teacher Expectations: The self-fulfilling prophecy in ghetto education'. *Harvard Educational Review*, 40, 411–451.

Roeders, P. (1989), *The Coaching Classroom: Increasing school effectiveness by a child oriented, creatively based educational method*. Paper presented at the 12th International School Psychology Association (ISPA) Conference, Ljubljana, Slovenia, August 1989.

Rosenbaum, J.E. (1976), *Making Inequality: The hidden curriculum of high school tracking*. New York: Wiley.

Ross, J.M., Bunton, W.J., Evison, P. and Robertson, T.S. (1972), *A Critical Appraisal of Comprehensive Education*. London: NFER.

Ross, J.M. and Simpson, H.R. (1971), 'The National Survey of Health and Development: 2. Rate of school progress between 8 and 15 years and between 15 and 18 years'. *British Journal of Educational Psychology*, 4, 125–135.

Rowan, B. and Miracle, A.W. (1983), 'Systems of Ability Grouping and the Stratification of Achievement in Elementary Schools'. *Sociology of Education*, 56, 133–44.

Rudd, W.G.A. (1956), 'The Psychological Effects of Streaming by Attainment with Special Reference to a Group of Selected Children'. *British Journal of Educational Psychology*, 28, 47–60.

Rutter, M., Maughan, B., Mortimore, P. and Ouston, J. (1979), *Fifteen Thousand Hours: Secondary Schools and Their Effects on Children*. London: Open Books.

Sammons, P., Hillman, J. and Mortimore, P. (1995), *Key Characteristics of Effective Schools: A review of school effectiveness research*. London: Ofsted.

Sammons, P., Thomas, S. and Mortimore, P. (1997), *Forging Links: Effective Schools and Effective Departments*. London: Paul Chapman Publishing.

Sands, M.K. (1981a), 'Group Work: Time for re-evaluation'. *Educational Studies*, 7, 2.

— (1981b), 'Group Work in Science: Myth or reality'. *School Science Review*, 26, 221.

Sands, M.K. and Kerry, T. (eds.) (1982), *Mixed Ability Teaching*. London: Croom Hill.

Sandven, J. (1971), 'Causes of Lacking a Sense of Well-Being in School'. *Scandinavian Journal of Educational Research*, 15 (1), 21–60.

— (1972), 'Sense of Well-Being in School as Perceived by Students and Teachers'. *Scandinavian Journal of Educational Research*, 16 (4), 117–160.

Sarason, S. (1990), *The Predictable Failure of Educational Reform: Can we change before it's too late?* San Francisco: Jossey-Bass.

Scheerens, J., Nanninga, H.C.R. and Pellgrum, W.J. (1989), 'Generalizability of Instructional and School Effectiveness Indicators Across Nations: Preliminary results of a secondary analysis of the IEA second mathematics study'. In B.P.M. Creemers, T. Peters and D. Reynolds (eds.), *School Effectiveness and School Improvement, Proceedings of the second international congress, Rotterdam*. Lisse: Swets & Zeitlinger.

Schneider, J.M. (1989), 'Tracking: A national perspective'. *Equity and Choice*, Fall, 11–17.

Schools Council (1977), *Mixed Ability Teaching in Mathematics*. London: Evans/Methuen.

Schwartz, F. (1981), 'Supporting or Subverting Learning: Peer groups patterns in four tracked schools'. *Anthropology and Education Quarterly*, 12, 99–121.

Scottish Education Department Inspectors of Schools (1992a), *Using Ethos Indicators in Primary School Self-Evaluation: Taking account of the views of pupils, parents and teachers.* Edinburgh: Scottish Office Education Department.

— (1992b), *Using Ethos Indicators in Secondary School Self-Evaluation: Taking account of the views of pupils, parents and teachers.* Edinburgh: Scottish Office Education Department.

Scottish Office (1996), *Achievement for All: A report on selection within schools.* Edinburgh: HMSO.

Selmes, I. (1987), *Improving Study Skills.* London: Hodder & Stoughton.

Sharp, C., Osgood, J. and Flanagan, N. (1999), *The Benefits of Study Support: A review of opinion and research.* London: DfEE.

Skapsi, M.K. (1960), 'Ungraded Primary Reading Program: An objective evaluation'. *Elementary School Journal,* 61, 41–45.

Slavin, R.E. (1987a), 'Ability Grouping and Student Achievement in Elementary Schools: A best evidence synthesis'. *Review of Educational Research,* 57 (3), 293–336.

— (1987b), 'Grouping for Instruction, Equity and Effectiveness'. *Equity and Excellence,* 23 (1–2), 31–36.

— (1987c), 'Mastery Learning Re-considered'. *Review of Educational Research,* 57, 175–213.

— (1990a) 'Achievement Effects of Ability Grouping in Secondary Schools: A best evidence synthesis'. *Review of Educational Research,* 60, 471–490.

— (1990b), 'Co-operative Learning'. In C. Rogers and P. Kutnick, *The Social Psychology of the Primary School.* London: Routledge.

Slavin, R.E. and Karweit, N.L. (1985), 'Effects of Whole Class, Ability Grouped and Individualised Instruction on Mathematics Achievement'. *American Educational Research Journal,* 22 (3), 351–67.

Sloboda, J.A., Davidson, J.W. and Howe, M.J.A. (1994), 'Is Everyone Musical?' *The Psychologist,* 7 (8), 349–354.

Smith, D. and Tomlinson, S. (1989), *The School Effect.* London: Policy Studies Institute.

Sorenson, A.B. and Hallinan, M.T. (1986), 'Effects of Ability Grouping on Growth in Academic Achievement'. *American Educational Research Journal,* 22 (3), 351–367.

Steedman, J. (1980), *Progress in Secondary Schools*. London: National Children's Bureau.

— (1983), *Examination Results in Selective and Non-Selective Schools: Findings of the National Development Study*. London: National Children's Bureau.

Sternberg, R.J. (1984), 'Toward a Triarchic Theory of Human Intelligence'. *Behavioural and Brain Sciences*, 7, 269–315.

Sternberg, R.J. and Weil, E.M. (1980), 'An Aptitude-Strategy Interaction in Linear Syllogistic Reasoning'. *Journal of Educational Psychology*, 72, 226–34.

Stevenson, H. and Lee, S. (1990), 'Contexts of Achievement: A study of American, Chinese and Japanese children'. *Monographs of the Society for Research in Child Development*, 221 (55), 1–2. Chicago: University of Chicago.

Sukhnandan, L. and Lee, B. (1998), *Streaming, Setting and Grouping by Ability: A review of the literature*. Slough: NFER.

Sunday Times (1994), 'Labour Schools go Back to Basics'. *Sunday Times*, 18 December 1994.

Swing, S. and Peterson, P. (1982), 'The Relationships of Student Ability and Small-Group Interaction to Student Achievement'. *American Educational Research Journal*, 19, 259–274.

Tann, S. (1981), 'Grouping and Groupwork'. In B. Simon and J. Willcocks (eds.), *Research and Practice in the Primary Classroom*. London: Routledge & Kegan Paul.

Taylor, N. (1993), 'Ability Grouping and its Effect on Pupil Behaviour: A case study of a Midlands comprehensive school'. *Education Today*, 43 (2), 14–17.

Thompson, D. (1974), 'Non-streaming Does Make a Difference'. *Forum*, 16, 45–49.

Tibbenham, A., Essen, J. and Fogelman, K. (1978), 'Ability-Grouping and School Characteristics'. *British Journal of Educational Studies*, 26 (1), 8–23.

Times Educational Supplement (1996), 'Ulster's poor pupils denied grammar diet'. *TES*, 19 January 1996.

Tomlinson, S. (1987), 'Curriculum Option Choices in Multi-Ethnic Schools'. In B. Troyna (ed.), *Racial Inequality in Education*. London: Tavistock.

Topping, K. (1992), 'Co-operative Learning and Peer Tutoring'. *The Psychologist*, 5, 151–157.

Tough, P. (1977), *The Development of Meaning: A study of use of language*. London: Allen and Unwin.

Troman, G. (1988), 'Getting it Right: Selection and setting in a 9–13 years middle school'. *British Journal of Sociology of Education*, 9 (4), 403–22.

Troyna, B. (1992), 'Ethnicity and the Organisation of Learning Groups: A case study'. *Educational Research*, 34 (1), 45–55.

Troyna, B. and Siraj-Blatchford, I. (1993), 'Providing Support or Denying Access? The experiences of students designated as ESL and SN in a multi-ethnic secondary school'. *Educational Review*, 45 (1), 3–11.

Tuckman, B.W. and Bierman, M. (1971), cited in W. Winn and A.P. Wilson (1983), 'The Affect and Effect of Ability Grouping'. *Contemporary Education*, 54, 119–125.

Turney, A.H. (1931), 'The Status of Ability Grouping'. *Educational Administration and Supervision*, 17, 21–42, 110–127.

Useem, E. (1990), *Social Class and Ability Group Placement in Mathematics in the Transition to 7th Grade: The role of parent involvement*. Paper presented at the Annual Meeting of the American Educational Research Association, Boston, USA, 1990.

Vanfossen, B.E., Jones, J.D. and Spade, J. Z. (1987), 'Curriculum Tracking and Status Maintenance'. *Sociology of Education*, 60, 104–122.

Veenman, S. (1995), 'Cognitive and Noncognitive Effects of Multigrade and Multi-Age Classes: A best evidence synthesis'. *Review of Educational Research*, 65 (4), 319–381.

Walberg, H. J. (1984), 'Improving the productivity of America's schools'. *Educational Leadership*, 44 (1), 19–27.

Waxman, H.C., Wang, M.C., Anderson, K.A. and Walberg, H.J. (1985), 'Synthesis of Research on the Effects of Adaptive Education'. *Educational Leadership*, 43 (1), 27–29.

Webb, N. (1983), 'Predicting Learning from Student Interaction: Defining the interaction variable'. *Educational Psychologist*, 18, 33–41.

— (1985), 'Verbal Interaction and Learning in Peer Directed Groups'. *Theory Into Practice*, 24 (1), 32–9.

— (1991), 'Task-Related Verbal Interaction and Mathematics Learning in Small Groups'. *Journal of Research in Mathematics Education*, 22, 366–389.

Whipple, G.M. (1919), *Classes for Gifted Children*. Bloomington: Public School Publishing.

Whitburn, J. (2001), 'Effective Classroom Organisation in Primary Schools: Mathematics'. *Oxford Review of Education*, 27 (3), 411–428.

Wiliam, D. and Bartholomew, H. (2001), *The Influence of Ability Grouping Practices on Student Achievement in Mathematics*. Paper presented at the Annual Conference of the British Educational Research Association, 12–15 September, University of Leeds, UK.

Willig, C.J. (1963), 'Social Implications of Streaming in Junior Schools'. *Educational Research*, 5, 151–154.

Willis, P.L. (1977), *Learning to Labour: How working class kids get working class jobs*. Driffield: Nafferton.

Willms, J.D. (1986), 'Social Class Segregation and its Relationship to Pupils' Examination Results in Scotland'. *American Sociological Review*, 51, 224–241.

Willms, J.D. and Cuttance, P. (1985), 'School Effects in Scottish Secondary Schools'. *British Journal of Sociology of Education*, 6, 289–306.

Wilson, B.J. and Schmidts, D.W. (1978), 'What's New in Ability Grouping?' *Phi Delta Kappan*, 59, 535–536.

Winn, W. and Wilson, A.P. (1983), 'The Affect and Effect of Ability Grouping'. *Contemporary Education*, 54, 119–125.

Wragg, E.C. (ed.) (1984), *Classroom Teaching Skills: The research findings of the teacher education project*. London: Routledge.

Wright, C. (1987), 'Black Students – White Teachers'. In B. Troyna (ed.), *Racial Inequality in Education*. London: Tavistock.

Wright, C., Weekes, D. and McGlaughlin, A. (2000), *Race, Class and Gender in Exclusion from School*. London: Falmer Press.

Yeomans, A. (1983), 'Collaborative Groupwork in Primary and Secondary Schools: Britain and USA'. *Durham and Newcastle Research Review*, X (51), 99–105.